BE BUNDY - MY HORSE IS MY TEACHER

EMBRACING THE POWER OF PRESENCE AND INTROSPECTION

MERINDA SMITH

CONTENTS

Acknowledgments	ix
Introduction	xi
1. Bundy's story	1
2. Melanie	9
3. Magpie to Bundy Bear	16
4. Amanda	23
5. Tom	39
6. Australia	44
7. The farm	55
8. Relationships	64
9. Looking for a new horse	68
10. George	72
11. Continuous learning	75
12. Fear	79
13. Hayley's wisdom	89
14. Courage	97
15. Self Awareness	108
16. Voicing my fears	118
17. We are unique	121
18. Love and ego	133
19. Bundy keeps teaching	141
20. Emotional intelligence	147
21. Managing emotions	156
22. Taking the joy as it comes	163
23. Judy	168
24. Equine assisted learning	174
25. Accountability	183
26. Counselling with horses	187
27. Responsibility	191
28. Beliefs	195
29. Introvert versus extrovert	199
30. Interschool competition	206
31. Being together	223

32. Work	229
Author's Note.	236
Notes	239

COPYRIGHT © 2023 MERINDA SMITH

The rights of Merinda Smith to be identified as the author of the work has been asserted by her in accordance with the Copyright Act of Australia, 1968.

All rights reserved.

No part of this book may be reproduced or transmitted in any form or by any means, electronic or mechanical, including photocopying, recording or by any information storage and retrieval system, without prior permission in writing from the publisher.

For any enquiries or permissions, the publisher can be contacted at merinda_smith@bigpond.com

First published in Australia by Merinda Smith.

Cover image shows Kate Addison riding Bundy Bear.

First Print: 2023

ISBN [Paperback]: 978-0-6457985-0-0

This work is a piece of fiction that incorporates elements inspired by events from my own life. However, it is crucial to emphasise that any resemblance to real individuals, whether living or deceased, is purely coincidental and unintended.

The characters and their actions have been created and developed to serve the purpose of the story. While certain events may have been influenced by personal experiences, they have been fictionalised and altered to fit the narrative.

It is my intention to provide an entertaining and imaginative work that should not be construed as a reflection or representation of real people or their lives.

This book is dedicated to Bundy Bear, the horse who came into my life and transformed it in ways I could never have imagined. Your presence and wisdom have been a constant source of inspiration and healing, and I am honoured to have shared this journey with you. You have taught me so much about empathy, leadership, and patience, and I am forever grateful for the lessons you have taught me.

I would like to extend my deepest gratitude to my husband, whose unwavering support and encouragement helped me to pursue my passion for writing. Without his love, encouragement, and listening skills, this book would not have been possible. Thank you for being my rock and my inspiration every step of the way.

ACKNOWLEDGMENTS

To my dear friend and confidant, Amanda, for allowing me to use her name in this book, and to Jordan, whose unwavering belief in the power of Bundy Bear inspired me to keep writing, I am deeply grateful. Your support and encouragement have meant the world to me, and I am honoured to have you both in my life.

To my editor, whose insights and expertise helped me to shape this book into its final form, I am grateful for your dedication and guidance.

I am deeply grateful to my family and friends for their continued support, patience, and understanding throughout my writing journey. Your love and encouragement sustained me through the challenges and triumphs of the process, and I am blessed to have you all in my life.

And finally, to all the animals in my life, past and present, who have taught me so much about myself and the world around me, thank you for your love, wisdom, and presence. You are all a cherished part of my journey.

INTRODUCTION

Profound understanding is divined by delving into the history of an individual to grant the ability to peer deep into the very essence of their soul.

We stood together in the arena so that all the spectators could see us. Bundy Bear stood tall and proud with his ears pricked. Eight horses and their riders stood together, the winners for each class. This year the classes had over forty riders, and we had done it. Bundy and I had won our class at the South West Horse Trials. Like actually won the huge event, with all its hills, the large jumps, and the strong competition from the acclaimed riders in my class. It was no mean feat.

"And the winner is Amanda Cavendish and Bundy Bear," announced the PA as our class came up on the list. My whole being buzzed with excitement. I could feel Bundy's body quiver as if he too knew what we had accomplished.

The PA announcer continued on to the next five placings. The sponsor for our class came forward with the rug and placed it on Bundy's back. A blue rosette was placed on his bridle and I was given a glass trophy. I turned back to smile at Bundy and he looked so proud. As the cameras and phones started to click he turned his head, with his ears pricked forward; he looked just as if he was smiling.

INTRODUCTION

It was a huge moment in our life together.

Bundy had transformed my life. He has taught me to listen and communicate and helped me to discover the best version of myself.

It wasn't always about winning; for years it has been about achieving small things and being open to what he had to share. He changed my life when I needed it most through what he had to say. Although he speaks horse and I speak human, he taught me how to really listen and communicate.

For what felt like an eternity, I dedicated my every waking moment to the pursuit of victory in equestrian events. But despite my best efforts, something always seemed to hold me back from achieving that elusive "rug" - that symbol of triumph and glory that every rider dreams of. I began to realise that I needed to dive deeper, to unearth the secrets that lay beneath the surface of my relationship with my equine partner. It was only through this process of exploration and attunement that I was able to unlock the full potential of our connection.

Over the course of our journey together, I discovered so much about myself and the way that I approach the world. I learned to see the world through new eyes, to listen with a different set of ears, and to open my heart to the lessons that were waiting to be learned. And through it all, I discovered that the most valuable lesson of all was the power of true, deep listening. Listening not just with my ears, but with my entire being - with my eyes, my heart, my soul.

I share my story with the world not just to inspire others, but to remind us all of the incredible wisdom that animals have to share. When we take the time to stop and truly listen, we unlock a world of knowledge and insight that we might never have otherwise known. I want to share this story so that you can learn to do it too, and be amazed at what animals can teach you when you stop to listen.

This is the story of my horse and how he taught me so much about myself, and the world in which I live. He helped me to see beyond my immediate vision of what I saw as my life, and helped me to look at others in a way I never had. He helped me in my leadership and to

INTRODUCTION

feel. To truly understand that feeling and what it means. I share with you stories of how he helped me in so many ways, as I helped him to grow into the beautiful horse he is today. Most importantly, he gave me the time to practise learning patience.

As soon as you catch a glimpse of Bundy Bear, a wave of his raw, untamed power washes over you. He oozes a sense of dominant but gentle presence. He's not only visually striking, with his magnificent patches of black and white, but he exudes a presence that demands respect. During the summertime, when his fur is trimmed short, you'll notice that some of the black patches turn into a deep, rich black-brown. On his near side, you'll notice a striking patch of hair that takes on the appearance of a lady's face. The profile of her face, as if she's lying back and gazing up at the sky, is simply captivating. Sometimes, I can't help but marvel at the wisdom and knowingness that emanates from her image.

Bundy's breeding is stock horse mixed with Clydesdale.

Bundy Bear's black and white tail is thick and strong, black on the inside and white on the outside. Whilst he loves to be dirty in the paddock, when he goes out he absolutely loves a bath and to be made to look sparkling. His tail is the envy of many riders who wish their horse also had a thick glossy tail just like his. His mane grows along his neck in black and white patches that are long and thick. When plaited, it makes cute black and white baubles that seem to dance down his neck as he moves.

Bundy Bear stands tall at 16.3 hands, giving him a commanding presence. His width only adds to his striking appearance, making him all the more impressive to behold. Despite his powerful stature, Bundy's true nature is revealed once you get to know him. Soft and gentle, he exudes a loveable quality that draws people in and captures their hearts.

Bundy has taught me so much. As we grew and bonded together, I've learnt with his wisdom and from my own studies that everyone has a story to tell. Yet not everyone does. Often, what we show to the outer world is a shell that we've gained to protect ourselves. Only

INTRODUCTION

when you get to know the story behind that shell, does it make communicating with that person easier. My big lessons were learning to communicate with Bundy Bear, and for that I needed to find out more about his life.

BUNDY'S STORY

There are times when a special angel appears on the earth.
They don't come with a bang, just silently step forth.

As a colt, he roamed freely across a vast cattle station in outback South Australia. He galloped through the rugged terrain, feeling the heat and cold on his skin. His hooves grew tough as they carried him across the land. The station itself was breathtaking in its scale and beauty, with stunning sunsets illuminating the towering ridges of the Flinders Ranges. In the evenings, the air was filled with the sounds of birds settling in for the night, and the light but heady scent of lemon wafted from the gum trees that dotted the landscape.

Living in such an isolated place came with its challenges, particularly during droughts when medical care was scarce. The station covered thousands of square kilometres, with the nearest neighbours hundreds of kilometres away, and the nearest major town several days' travel. Despite the difficulties, however, he thrived in this environment and became a hardy and resilient creature, adapted to the rugged beauty of the outback.

Long before Bundy Bear was born, the station owners brought Clydesdales[1] over from Scotland, to help the station owners work the land. It was said by people who seemed to know, that a selection of quality stallions and mares were brought to Australia from Scotland where they were bred as versatile draught horses for farm work, coal mining, and heavy haulage. Their high step, originally used to navigate rough terrain and pull ploughs, now sets them apart from other horses and is a notable feature of their appearance. Clydesdales have a rich history and continue to be respected for their strength and beauty.

The station had a few Clydesdale stallions and one that was a descendant of the original horses who had ploughed the paddocks. These were bred with station mares that may have had thoroughbred and mountain pony bloodlines. Whilst the original horses have long since gone, the incredible genes that made them strong and resilient were passed down to all the foals. They were known for being very gentle, easy going, and trainable horses that were a joy to work with.

The stock on the station were bred to be sold each year which added to the station income. At the end of winter every year, a new set of foals would be born to the mares. The foals, would stay with the mares and the main herd for six to nine months, roaming the vast paddocks. Then they would be separated from their mothers and left together in a large paddock to bond, grow and mature - the fillies in one paddock and the colts in another.

Growing up in this environment, Bundy Bear learnt about the sounds and smells of the open bush, which plants to eat, the power of connection, love, and of being himself. He learnt that the sun rises over the hills in the east, and that sunsets disappeared quickly across the plains to the west. He saw kangaroos, emus, lizards, and snakes as they moved along and got on with their business. He depended on his herd to survive and learnt about relationships, the magic of trusting others, and having the courage to be free. Bonding with members of the heard and having a sense of belonging made Bundy's life special.

In a herd that was mostly brown, his mixture of black and brown splotches on a white body, along with the white face and white legs, made him very striking. Deep in his soul he sensed there was something special about him, but he didn't know what it was, or why he felt that way. He was not an arrogant horse, he was very humble, and always interested in his fellow horses. He never did anything to bring attention to himself, yet when others spent time with him, there was a spark, a connection, a joy in his soul that told you he was glad to be with you.

The station experience and being with a large herd living on hundreds of acres, allowed him to appreciate the values of being in a horse herd. He learnt that an essential part of communication and dynamics between the members was to be influential, yet sensitive; to be wise and establish clear boundaries. The subtleties of horse language were instilled at birth, along with the rough and tumble, where horses were being pushed and moved about with an obvious kick and bite as a horse shared his thoughts and demanded his space. Or other times slight gestures of an ear, or head moved them. Similarly, there were times when a snort or a toss of a head would warn of approaching danger. Just like children, there also were the playful movements, short snorts or squeals that sounded like laughter, lots of fun with dust flying and giant bodies arching and thumping. In all this movement was a deliberate regularity to the behaviour, to bring the herd safety, peace, joy, and success.

One thing all these working horses had in common was their heavy horse breeding. This made for heavier legs, and footfalls that were heard as they hit the ground. In fact, you could even feel the ground vibrating when some of these heavy-footed horses would get to run for a muster! These horses were designed to carry 120kgs of men, complete with long booted legs, spurs, felt hats, moustaches and 40kgs of roping saddle with assorted saddlebags. Yet even with the heavy feet, they were quite cat-like as they darted back and forth gathering stock that had gotten away. They were sure of where each foot went as they galloped through the bush. They spun on a dime, jumped fallen logs, and loved their job, knowing just when to move, sometimes, even before the rider knew! Riders and horses were often seen walking across the paddocks with no contact on their mouths or reins; the riders rolling cigarettes, or speaking to another alongside them. These horses were the salt of the earth and loved by all who rode them.

The stockmen on the station were tough. They pulled down bullocks, brandished hot branding irons, swore like any trouper, yet were very capable of talking quietly with sick, stressed, or injured animals. They demanded as much from their horses as themselves and their ability as riders.

In the early hours of the morning, during a week of hot days, the stock horses were prepared for a muster. The head stockman was told it would be a long mustering as they would be bringing the wild colts in from the far paddock. The plan was to bring the colts to the place called 'dry creek' where the horsemen would hold the wild horses for up to forty-five minutes to settle them and let the younger ones catch their breath. Bringing the wild horses in by mustering on horseback was necessary for them to have a settled herd when they got to the homestead.

The day was going well as the sun rose high in the sky and the horses came into 'dry creek'. The nine stockmen had rounded up about a hundred head of horses, including the younger weanlings, and the much targeted two-year-olds. After a rest and some water, the herd and riders walked on towards the yards by the homestead, some three hours away. The going was slow, as the heat had really started to beat down. Slowly they made their way towards the next yards, but even at a walking pace, sweat poured off the riders and horses alike.

It was early afternoon by the time the mob was brought into the yards. Water troughs were filled, and the entire herd was penned together for the night. Having them all together stopped them from having the space to rush in the yard overnight, and the possibility of busting out of the yard, as they had done on many occasions when they had too much room. The colts were entire, and the testosterone in the older ones would sometimes cause havoc, which in turn could cause a huge crushing of the horses.

Even when the cooler night air came in, which in most cases seemed to settle the horses, this time it didn't. The horses yelled out and bit and kicked one another in the confines of the yards. The stockmen turned their backs and hoped they would eventually settle and be ready for the drafting work the following morning.

As the muster horses were washed down and fed for the day, the horses in the yard continued to squeal and thuds could be heard across the land as one, then two horses would lash out at others. The smell of sweat and dust hung in the air.

In contrast, the muster horses were let out into a holding paddock ready for another big day. They would be walking the horses that were too young to be sold back to their paddock after drafting was finished the following day. The stockmen, tired and hungry from the day's work, headed home and prepared for another early start of drafting the following day.

As the sun rose the next morning, so did the stockmen. The cook was already up and prepared the open fire and cooked the food with simple utensils, including a tin billy[2] which was used as a cooking pot or to boil water. They breakfasted on mutton chops and eggs, and drank hot black tea boiled in the billy. The flies had started to buzz, and they were already getting into the eyes of the stockmen as they ate their fill. They needed to commence the drafting of the two-year-old horses, so they were separated from the rest of the mob before the sun got too hot.

Walking down to the yard, the men scratched themselves and yawned to the sound of snorting horses, and stomping feet that rid the flies that landed on them. As they looked around the yard, it was quieter than when they had left the night before, but there seemed to be some horses lying down in the middle that hadn't risen with the sun. The stockmen climbed the yard fence to see if they could see what had happened, but all the horses rushed to the other side and created such a barrier, nothing could be seen.

It could take a couple of hours to draft the horses, and then they needed to get the main mob back to their paddock, so they had to get going. They decided to start the draft and as the yard cleared, they would see what was happening with the horses they had seen on the ground.

As they got started, it became apparent that a bay colt had been kicked and wasn't able to stand on all four legs anymore. One of the others stood by, and it appeared that one colt had swelling in his leg, yet could still walk. The stockmen moved the horses out of the yard as quickly as they could, so they could examine the injured wild-eyed colt. As one of the wiry experienced stockmen approached him, he tried to stand, revealing a swarm of thick flies on his front leg. When he moved, the wound revealed a bad cut down to the bone; then the flies covered the cut once again.

"He won't be walking anywhere today," said the stockman. "A horse with only three legs is useless to anyone. Those flies will cause it to go septic within a couple of hours. There is no way we can patch that leg with him being so wild. Take the one with the swelling and put it with the mob, let's hope he can walk back slowly with them. Fill the water trough and give the other bugger some hay, we'll come back for him with the truck once we're finished with the others," he barked out orders as he strode off to saddle his horse.

Later than they had hoped, but successful after two- and a-bit hours, the herd was split into two. Some of the horses would remain on the property, and some would be sold off at a sale yard.

This time there were seventeen colts that were suitable to be readied for sale. It was a good season, and it brought some good-looking youngsters. There was one colt, a black and white one that stood out from the rest. Not only did he have striking colouring, he had the *je ne sais quoi* about him, which made him very appealing. He and the other youngsters were left with fresh water and some hay whilst the men took the mob back to the main paddock that looked across the ranges. The young horses, cantered around the yards as the others were driven from their enclosure, creating dust and tension and covering their coats in sweat. The sound of horses being separated from each other filled the air for the next few hours; men yelling and horses neighing for their friends.

As the stockmen returned to the yards, the colts were prepared for a new life outside of the herd. For the next six weeks all of them were 'broken in' so that they could be ridden, branded, gelded and drenched by the station stockmen.

Many of the stockmen were exceptional horsemen, and well recognised for their talent to 'break a horse'[3] and the ability to mitigate from the danger it entailed.

It was said that the Aboriginal riders were the kindest. They respected the horses, and listened to their needs, rather than pushing through with demands. When these people worked with the horses, it was more like horse whispering. Over the campfires at night, they would share stories from thousands of years; dreamtime stories of the land and how it came to be. Sadly, there were only a few who worked quietly like this, so mostly the six weeks were full of wild bucking from the horses, and riders clinging to the saddles to stay on. The days were hot and long, filled with the smell of sweat, dust, the flies, pain, and fear.

The black and white colt was amongst them, and he saw and felt it all. The pain ran through the small herd in both a physical sense and spiritually. He watched as horse after horse put up a fight and lost. He noticed one of the horses was continually arguing back. He would put up fights with his handler and the other horses. Different stockmen would try to work him, but his fighting was unrelenting. And he would not succumb to the new ways of having a saddle and rider on his back. At the end of the week, one of the stockmen was told to lead the horse that 'can't be 'broken' away from the station and the other horses, and to release him. This horse was of no use to the station, and they didn't need him. To a horse that would mean certain death, being isolated and alone.

After six weeks of saddling, riding and working the young horses they were ready, having passed their basic training. The job was thorough so that the station held its valued reputation for quality horses and preparation. Their 'breaking in' was complete and they were ready for their next adventure. Horse from this station made good money when sold. Early Tuesday morning, at the end of the six weeks, all the newly broken horses were loaded onto a big open road train[4] as they prepared to go to the city sale yards. The road train and its metal cages were to be their home for the next day and a half.

The truck with horses travelled the dusty, rocky roads and main highways into Adelaide, the capital of South Australia, where they would be sold. The horses were cramped together for that whole time. There were two drivers in the prime mover cab. One would drive, whilst the other slept in the bed at the back of the seats, which meant they could drive all day and all night long. They only stopped at roadhouses for ablutions, and to get some food and drink. The horses would have access to water but due to the cramped conditions, hay would only be given once they arrived. As they travelled the highways towards Adelaide, the air cooled, and the heat from the outback turned into balmy spring weather.

The horses from White Tree Station were destined for the stockyard, where Crucial Sales took place every two months on the third Thursday. The bidding began at 10am and the sales were renowned for their high-quality horses, which attracted a large number of buyers. The truck carrying the horses was headed towards the Crucial Sales located on the outskirts of the city.

Upon arrival at the sale yards the day before the sales, there were numerous horses of varying shapes and sizes being put into the yards. The horses from White Tree Station were so excited to be out of the confined space and allowed to stretch their legs that they bucked and kicked out as they left the truck.

As the horses entered the yards, they were separated and given a number that was tied to their mane. They were then provided with water and hay to ensure their needs were met.

The next day, Thursday, started early as people and dogs started to arrive to check out the horses before the bidding started. In Adelaide, this public auction was one of the main venues for buying and selling horses. At these yards future stars changed ownership quickly. It was well known in riding circles that if you wanted a horse you would find a good range of horses to choose from, at the sales, and sometimes at great prices.

MELANIE

Seeking something for you by seeking what others want for you.
Never ends in success.
Over time without actually knowing who you are
You repeat similar patterns of failure.
Learning from your mistakes is the path of growth.

Melanie Smithers had come to the yards to find her next horse. She was a competent rider, yet she craved a project horse, one who would take her up the ranks of dressage.[1] She told her girlfriend she was on the lookout for her next forever horse and needed to move onto a decent size. Something over 15.3hh.[2]

Since she was six, Melanie and her sister had attended Pony Club, where they shared a pony. In her early teens, her sister had given up riding and Melanie had the pony all to herself. When Melanie had outgrown the pony, she had leased a couple of horses and ridden them at dressage competitions. Not having much money to spend on her new horse, she believed she might be able to snag a bargain at a sale yard. As a child she had often attended these auctions with her father, who would buy a young horse, train it up and then sell it for a high price. Although her father had passed away, Melanie was determined to find her next "forever" horse at the next available auction.

The next day started early as people, and their dogs began to arrive to check out the horses before the bidding started. In Adelaide, this public auction was one of the main venues for buying and selling horses. It was well known in riding circles that if you wanted a horse, you would find a range of horses to choose from and sometimes at great prices.

Missing her father and his valuable horse knowledge, she arrived early to prepare herself for the horses on offer. She brought her 4 x 4 ute and float, in anticipation of finding the right kind of horse. As she stretched her long legs out of the ute, she smelt the horse sweat in the crisp morning air, heard the snorts and whinnies of horses calling out to each other, and spied some of the beautiful beats in the yards. "Very impressive, and huge range of all colours, shapes and sizes," she thought. "Dad would love to see these beauties." Melanie knew she needed a big horse, to carry her long legs, so any ponies were out.

She walked the yards looking up and down at all the horses. She was excited at the prospect of buying a new horse, and tried to keep her bouncing feet under control.

"Boy, this is hard!" she thought to herself. "How am I going to know which horse to buy? Dad, you need to help me out here," she said looking at the sky.

There were the thoroughbred type horses, tall, slim, and sleek. There were the stock horses who were smaller and yet heavier in body weight. Then there were a number of horses who looked like they were crossbred with a draught breed. She wanted a gelding,[3] as she had been taught that the mares had a 'catty' nature, and it had been impressed upon her that geldings were known to have a reliable temperament.

Melanie's father had been a firm believer that geldings made better mounts. According to his philosophy, they were safer and easier to train, plus didn't come with the "moody mare baggage," as he called it. "With a gelding, you always know which horse you're taking out of the paddock," he'd say. "With a mare, you never know."

As an adult, Melanie had heard variations of this wisdom from other horse owners, too, so she considered the merits of their experience. People confirmed that geldings tended to have fewer mood swings than mares because they have no seasonal cycles. However, she found it was usually those with geldings who would swear they were better than mares. But mare owners would stick up for their choices, too.

It was warm and sunny that first day of spring, with new growth sprouting everywhere. Spring signals fresh beginnings, and for Melanie, she hoped it would be a fresh start for her too. She walked up to a young-looking horse and looked into its eye. Melanie's heart ached as she stood at the auction, still grieving the loss of Cocoa, her beloved pony of twenty years; she had buried him just a week prior. Her heart ached, and she felt like no one else could possibly understand the deep pain within her soul.

As Cocoa had got older, and Melanie too had gotten older and bigger, she knew he was too small for her, yet she still loved him deeply and hadn't been ready to give him up. He stayed with her for all his final years. Even as a senior, he was a healthy horse and was able to be ridden once a week until his mid-twenties. As he got older, his diet changed, and he was given extra rugs to keep him warm, but he remained her best friend till the day he died. She knew she certainly was not the first, nor would she be the last to lose a beloved horse friend, and she decided a new mount would sooth her soul.

Melanie shrugged and brought herself back to the present moment. She registered herself as a bidder and got her yellow number and a catalogue, so that she knew more about the horses as they went around. She wanted to see the horses close up, and then when they were out moving. That way she had a better understanding of their conformation and the likely hood of any issues.

The horses stood in the yards with numbers on their backs, so that you knew which one they were.

Moving on from the young horse, with the catalogue in her hand, she decided she needed a coffee. A coffee would stop her from being so sad and would awaken her senses. Stuffing the catalogue into her jeans back pocket she looked for a food van, or canteen. Whilst she couldn't see a stall close by, she spied someone eating a roll that appeared to have egg dripping out of it.

"Yum" she thought. "Bacon and egg butty. Perfect, just what I need - that and a coffee." She strode off in the direction of where the person had come from, in search of her sustenance. The search took longer than expected, but finally she found the area and stood in line to order. As she waited, she looked at the others around her. There were city types, and country folk, people who had lived hard, and others with shiny RM Williams boots, and clean cream moleskin trousers. Melanie smiled to herself at how horses could bring such a diverse group of people together.

After enjoying her hot roll and coffee, she set out to find her next horse. As she walked around the yard, she couldn't help but consider what her father would have said about each of the horses she saw. She was certain he would have assessed them based on their appearance - the look in their eye, their colour, size, age, and breed. As she continued her stroll, she came across a medium sized chestnut horse that didn't particularly stand out from the others, but she was drawn to his kind eye. She thought to herself, Dad would be pleased with this one, as he lifted his head and sniffed her hand. "Hello," she said to him and allowed him time to sniff.

The catalogue didn't provide much information about him - not his past, nor his age. She tried to check his teeth to get an idea of his age, but he pulled away, and she couldn't get close enough. Despite the lack of information, she still liked the look of him and decided to take a chance. With a smile on her face, she marked a smiley face next to his number in her catalogue as she walked away noting that he was due up for auction in a couple of hours.

It was time to look at the catalogue and see if anything took her fancy. She decided to sit down and go through it properly. Finding a small table and bench she sat down and commenced her perusal. She was distracted by the sound of hooves moving around and looked up to see a small group of heavier horses being taken from their yards and trotted around. She was intrigued. They had great paces, and even lifted their feet up high. She liked the look of those horses and their gait.

Then as she watched, a black and white horse was paraded in front of her. He held his head high and had a certain magic quality about him. He seemed to look at everyone, and yet focused on Melanie. As he passed, she swore she saw him eyeball her, prick his ears and even thought she saw a smile on his face. Melanie berated herself for even thinking he would smile, but kept looking at him. She was taken by his markings and even thought she saw the shape of a woman's face on one of his sides. His legs were good and solid, which would make him good for riding. His hooves looked strong, and well-shaped. She could see his strength, yet also a softness and a vulnerability.

She looked around and saw a few others watching. Everyone's eye was drawn to this horse – as if he was a movie star. Melanie had a good feeling about him, and decided she needed to keep an eye on him as well. Still only young, he was the horse Melanie imagined herself sitting on in perfect balance, travelling across the land in style. She noted the horses had come from a station up north and thought that was a good sign as they would be hardy.

Taking note of the number 290 stuck on his mane, she looked around to see if he had elicited any attention and sure enough she saw others watching him with interest. Well aware that she only had a small budget, she waited patiently for the horses to come to the stage and her turn to bid. Horses were selling at huge prices that day, and many were going for much more than she expected. The nondescript chestnut horse she had looked at earlier came up and sold for a huge price; far beyond what she was prepared to pay. Someone else had seen those kind eyes, too, she thought. She looked at the other horses and wondered if she would be able to find her new friend today. The sun had gotten hot, and it was beginning to look like she had wasted her time coming out.

Feeling like she had let her father down she walked to the yards again to familiarise herself with the ones that were-left. She smiled as she saw that the striking black and white heavy horse was still there, so she decided to stay and hang around until it was his turn.

As she sat waiting and hoping, she imagined how she would be riding this horse and how he would float over the ground and arch his neck - his head held high and his mane sweeping across the sky as they galloped together. With those thoughts came the realisation that she couldn't turn her back on him now, she was committed and maybe even in love. When finally, late in the afternoon the black and white horse came out, many of the buyers had left and there were only a few people left to bid.

Feeling discombobulated, she walked down to the yards again to familiarise herself with the ones that were left. She vowed to herself that coming home empty-handed was not a failure. So many needed new homes, and her bleeding heart called out to her to buy them all. But she simply couldn't bring them *all* home. The last thing she wanted was to get attached to a hopeless case that would end up costing her a fortune in vet bills before she had to put it out of its misery anyway.

She so wanted that total gem – a diamond in the rough and she knew there were bargains to be had at auctions. She smiled as she saw that the striking black and white heavy horse was still there, so she decided to stay and wait until it was his turn. As she sat waiting and hoping, she imagined how she would be riding this horse and how he would float over the ground and arch his neck. With these thoughts came the realisation that she couldn't turn her back on him now. When finally late in the afternoon the black and white horse came out into the auction yard, many of the buyers had left and there were only a few people left to bid.

As he walked nervously around the yard, the auctioneer started the bidding, "So this number 290, a black and white from a station up north. 200, 200 we ask," he looked around the shed and someone started the bid.

"200 we bid today," he shouted, pointing towards Melanie.

"Look at this 220," He said, pointing over at a man in a red jacket.

"230, behind me now, 240 in front, 250," he pointed to someone else on the other side whom Melanie couldn't see.

The offers were slow in coming, and for a while she thought she might get a bargain. Then the bidding picked up. "350 to you Madam," shouted the auctioneer, "370, behind me now, 390 to you Madam" and Melanie got caught in the bidding.

"400" shouted the auctioneer when someone placed another bid to counter hers, and Melanie almost gave up. But she looked across at the horse and knew she couldn't. It was as if her father was saying, "do it,"

"Last call, at 400" and Melanie shot her card in the air.

"420" he shouted, and jammed down the hammer on her bid. "Thank you Madam and your number is…?" as Melanie showed him her number she knew she had paid more than she had expected to, but realised she still had a bargain.

She had a new friend, and the horse had a new home.

MAGPIE TO BUNDY BEAR

Destiny shares new life, new challenges and new stories.

She was excited as she loaded him onto her float with the help of one of the marshals and took him up the winding roads to the hills of Adelaide and his new home. Melanie had a small plot of land near Hahndorf, next to some wineries in the Adelaide Hills. She wanted to ride him at shows, to do dressage, and maybe some small jumps. To Melanie he was a very handsome horse, with his colouring and unique markings, and she suspected he would draw much attention. As she drove him home, she imagined riding him to events, and cleaning up all the prizes!

Once she got him home, she named him Magpie, because of his black and white colouring, and the similarity of the magpie birds that surrounded her small five-acre lot. Due to the shortage of feed on her place, she had a kept the horses in small yard like paddocks. Magpie was placed in a small, railed paddock all by himself; her older horse was nearby, but not close enough to smell, or reach out and touch.

Magpie had a tall gum tree for shelter, one that he found strangely familiar, with that minty, sweet, camphor scent. Its pungent smell would waft through the air in the cooler mornings, and the shade from it would soothe him during the hot days. The smell reminded him of times gone by, and that strange familiarity gave him comfort. A flock of magpie birds would come and sit in the tree and eat the worms on the ground. He got used to their cries as they gathered the family together. His yard was watered with a tall sprinkler that would be turned on during the day to keep the grass green. Little wren like birds would come and stand on his back as he walked the perimeter of the small fence. From the outside looking in, you would think Magpie would be happy with all that green grass, watering and shelter. Yet there was something missing from his life.

From the moment he arrived, he was ridden every day by Melanie; something he was not used to. He was pushed and pulled into directions he'd never known before. He was a young and resilient horse, so he tried his best. He truly wanted to please, but it didn't seem to work.

Magpie, like many horses from stations, enjoyed having ample space and the company of other horses. However, he found himself confined to a smaller space without the presence of his companions, which made him unhappy. Despite complying with his rider's requests, he still longed for the freedom he once had, along with the comfort of his friends and family. His yearning for his herd was immense, and though he understood that he needed to trust his new rider, he found himself resisting. He would often stand alone for hours with one hind leg resting, staring off into space. His individuality was gradually being suppressed, and he was becoming increasingly withdrawn.

The feeling seemed to be reciprocated, and even after only a short six months, Melanie was not feeling the love with her equine partner. She had tried, but it just wasn't to be, he didn't' seem to fit her mould of the perfect horse she had in her mind. The beautiful Magpie had never done anything wrong either, they just weren't a match. Melanie asked her best friend Tanya to look him over and watch as she rode him. She trusted Tanya's opinion, and before she did anything rash like selling him, she wanted to be sure he wasn't right for her.

She trotted Magpie around the arena, and he raised his head high, sticking his neck out. His easy going gait was stiff and whilst he didn't show signs of lameness, he wasn't looking his best.

"Take him over these trotting poles," said Tanya.

Melanie trotted him down the poles and his movement loosened, yet Melanie wasn't happy with how he was going. Rider and horse seemed to argue together, one pulling one way and the other pulling in another direction. It seemed like it was a constant battle against wills.

"So, what is the real issue here, Melanie?" asked Tanya.

"I think, if I'm honest with myself, we just don't have that feeling. I feel like I'm riding a stiff board, and he overreacts to me and what I ask of him," replied Melanie.

"Over time, he would make a great horse," said Tanya.

"Not for me though, I'm just not feeling it," said Melanie.

"Too bad," came Tanya's reply.

"That's the breaks of buying form a sale yard."

"He really is a good-looking horse though," reflected Tanya, "Maybe you could get your money back and some. Have you considered selling him online?"

"You're right, I could go online and the whole of Australia can see him. Someone will fall for his good looks," said Melanie.

"There's those deals one, what's it called?" asked Tanya.

"Oh yes, 'online equine deals' I think it is, let me take a look when I get inside," said Melanie.

"Do you want me to take some pictures whilst we have him saddled up, I could do one of you jumping him," said Tanya.

"Yes, great idea, let's do that now," replied Melanie.

The girls went about taking loads of photos in preparation to sell Magpie. The online site was national and sold some impressive horses. He fitted in perfectly.

Within hours of uploading the listing, Melanie had enquiries from people all over the country. Many of them wanted him without even meeting him. She figured it was just like being at an auction; you don't actually know what you are getting. In the end, she narrowed the prospective buyers down to someone in Western Australia, and someone in Queensland. The Queensland lady wanted to do reining with him, where he would chase bulls in a yard, whilst the man in WA wanted him for his son to compete in dressage and jumping.

On a hot day in September, Melanie took him to a racing stable yard where she was to meet a truck that transports horses across the country. He was loaded into a stall on the side, and she waved goodbye to him as the truck left the stables for their next pick-up. He travelled across the country on the horse truck, and it took days to get to Western Australia.

However, once they had arrived safely, life became intolerable for poor Magpie. His riders were big and strong, and demanded a lot from their horses. They rode the horses using their strength and demanded compliance. Riding, to them, was about influencing a horse to do what they wanted. There was no art to their riding, whereas with other riders the horse could be working in partnership under a whisper or even without being asked. These boys used their strength as their weapon.

Poor Magpie was whipped repeatedly in an attempt to train him to behave properly. He was whipped to make him jump higher, and his mouth was pulled to make him stop. However, instead of becoming more obedient, this training method actually made him resistant, disobedient, and unresponsive to his rider's commands.

His resistance and disobedience meant it took more brute force for them to force him to do what they wanted. When the riders whacked him with the whip, it would sting and incite Magpie into reacting; so naturally, he would reply with a buck or pigroot, where his hind legs would go skywards with the intent to dislodge his rider. To Magpie, it was a perfectly reasonable response to the irritation of the rider and his whip. The pig rooting became a viable answer to relieve the sting of the whip and the continual pressure that was exerted on him, and he used this response on a regular basis. Within that stable yard he became known as a "rogue"; a horse that needed a firm hand. He was called the Rogue by all at the stable hands but continued to be called Magpie on his entry forms.

As winter settled in, Magpie's long, flowing coat grew out and made him look absolutely stunning. His thick, hairy coat stuck to everything, including his rider, saddle cloth, and even himself. Despite his impressive appearance, this extra coat wasn't ideal for a horse that needed to jump and run around. With all that hair, Magpie could easily overheat or become too cold if he wasn't dried off quickly. He needed to be clipped. But before that happened, Magpie was expected to demonstrate his obedience and cooperation.

That night, the crew of grooms and riders sat around the campfire drinking, eating and chatting about the next day's ride. As they chatted, the boys decided they didn't like the name Magpie for the hairy 'rogue' horse. Sitting around the fire, warming themselves against the cold breeze, and drinking rum, they tossed around names.

"Blacky," was one suggestion from a moustached man. Then more people chimed in, and soon the names were flowing in the air.

"Fluffy" came out with a giggle, "Hairy" came another.

"He looks like a bear with all that hair," said Jenny, one of the stable girls as she rubbed her hands together, blowing into them to warm them up from the cold. "It's so long and gets everywhere." She picked a white hair from her glove, then leant over to fill up her glass. She grabbed the rum bottle and looked hard at the label, as she poured another drink.

"What about Bundy Bear?" uttered another girl as she watched the stable hand eye the bottle of rum. Her long red hair, and matching red beanie was topped by a white pompom that bounced as she spoke. She moved forward and asked for the bottle from the stable hand.

"What?" said the man with a black beanie jammed over his ears. Pointing to the logo on the bottle she repeated, louder this time, "Bundy Bear"? They all laughed and agreed. It was decided he looked like the bear on the logo on the rum bottle– a big fat polar bear called Bundy. The name stuck, and the next event he was entered into, he was called "Bundy Bear".

Being a big horse, Bundy Bear could use his size to push back at the riders so that he could try and stay safe, just like he'd seen done by other horses in his herd. When he was whipped, he'd kick out, when he was told to run, he'd run fast to try and get away from the pain. He resisted with all his might, wanting to get away from the distress. He was confused, and so he tried doing just as his riders were doing. He pulled hard against their hands, he pushed his 600kg size against them when they were on the ground, or on top of him, riding. He tried to run from the discomfort, and he would gallop with his rider on top; his aim was to protect himself. All of this caused more pain, more frustration, and less understanding.

In the stable yard, the two riders continued to call him the rogue and thought of him as just another horse, something to ride and compete at events, so that they could win. They knew he had the potential, and once he started to win, they could earn their money. They were big men who were strong and hard. Neither gave him any special attention.

As the night settled in, Bundy found solace in his dreams. He yearned to be with someone who treated him with kindness and respect. Though he enjoyed being a riding horse and meeting other horses at shows, he despised the way he was treated at his current stable. Deep down, he held onto the belief that one day he would find a home where he would be truly happy. This hope was what kept him going, day after day. Despite the discomfort and pain of being ridden, Bundy was able to bear it as long as he could dream of a better future.

When he went to competitions, he would look at the other riders and hope. He wished he could find someone who loved him. He would watch the other horses and marvel at how they were connected with their riders. He knew there was another way, but he had no idea how to change what he was going through.

In the quiet hours of the day Jenny, the stable girl, would give him a scratch, or brush him down, and talk to him. She liked him and he came to trust and like her. She was kind and soft when she was around him and treated him like her special horse. Jenny would sometimes ride the horses to get them fit for their competitions, yet she didn't have any need for Bundy Bear to jump high, nor compete and win ribbons, so she never forced him to do anything. Her job was to keep the horses fit, and that mostly meant lots of trotting. Occasionally, she would take them over small jumps, just to keep their muscles strong. That lack of pressure was soothing to Bundy's soul. Whilst she loved all the horses in the yard, she especially loved Mr. Bear for his colouring. She was a soft and considerate rider and when she rode him, he felt lighter.

Over their time together, he started to learn that being ridden didn't need to be hard and forced. He knew from those brief rides that there was another way to be with a human, and it could be good, built on love and trust. He savoured those days when she would ride him, but as she only worked in the yard three days a week, it wasn't often. So, in the two years in the eventing yard there was more pushing and pulling than love and trust.

Bundy Bear was a strong horse, and he always did his best, but it seemed he couldn't escape the mistreatment he received. Whenever he was frightened, he would knock down the rails from the show jumping fences, which resulted in him being whipped by his rider. He became scared of the whipping and tried to outrun the pain. In eventing, the goal was to have the lowest score possible, and each mistake incurred a penalty. Bundy's score suffered because of the penalties he received from knocking down rails, and despite his potential to win events, he was never very successful.

After a while, the men who owned him lost hope that Bundy would submit to their ways, so they decided to sell him. Unfortunately, with no wins to his name, he could only be sold based on his potential, and he wasn't the great sale they had hoped for.

AMANDA

A small package bouncing with zest for life.
Changed by trying to fit in, squashed by teachers, peers.

I grew up as a normal teenager from a normal family of four children, living in a normal house, having a normal life. Well, that's what it looked like from the outside.

Deep within me, there existed a reservoir of tender emotions, but unfortunately, my older siblings, who were in their teenage years, created obstacles that prevented me from expressing them freely. Rather than displaying acts of brotherly love, their actions often felt hostile, and their words were sometimes downright mean-spirited. They took pleasure in mocking and teasing me, taking advantage of the fact that I was six years younger. They never treated me as an equal, nor did they engage in any playful activities with me. Every attempt I made to establish a connection with them was met with resistance.

To them, I was nothing more than an annoyance, someone who always got in the way and spoiled their enjoyment. But what they didn't understand was that I just wanted to be part of their lives.

Then there was Margaret, my sister.

My sister, Margaret, who was three years my senior, had excelled at everything she touched. She was kind, she was funny, she won athletics and swimming trophies, and she was gorgeous looking.

I am short and slim built but not pretty, I know that. No one said to me, "Gosh you're stunning," or "you would make a future model," as they did to Margaret. The kind aunts would come to our house, look me up and down, and say things like, "it's all right, maybe you'll have the brains in the family".

But when Margaret went to the University of Western Australia and studied Medicine, I realised that even in the brains department, she won out. The delight on my mother's face was unconscionable as she told everyone how proud she was of Margaret and her achievements.

My parents always gave me the impression I was just not doing the right thing by them, or whatever standards they were upholding. I tried to meet the family standards, but it seemed that I had not been consulted along this journey, and I always felt I was trying to be everyone else. At school, I tried to fit in, I pushed myself to talk more, to laugh more and join in the team sports. But I wasn't a sporting person. It seemed I was all arms and legs that didn't coordinate together. During the first season, I was whistled off the netball and basketball court so often, that there was no point in me even being on the team. I went along to support and cheer the others on, but as the season went on, I found excuses to not go. Eventually, I stopped pretending and just didn't turn up.

When my sister was introduced to friends, or new acquaintances by my parents, I watched as their eyes shone bright, and their mouths would display a wide smile. When it came to my turn to be introduced, I was often left out, so I would have to introduce myself, or my mother would flick a wrist in my direction to indicate that I existed but was irrelevant.

I was quiet and kept to myself, I didn't want to stand out.

The reality was I just wasn't my sister.

While my sister was out enjoying parties and balls hosted by the local rural youth club, I was always left behind. Instead of being allowed to join in the fun, I was confined to my room under the pretence of preparing for events that may or may not happen.

I didn't think it was unfair or unreasonable to want to attend the occasional party with my friends, but I was never given the chance. It felt like I was being punished for no reason, and I couldn't understand why my parents were so against me socialising with my peers.

I longed to be out in the world, experiencing new things and making new friends, but instead, I was left feeling isolated and alone. It was a difficult time for me, but I held onto the hope that someday my parents would see things differently and let me spread my wings.

Not everyone gets those tall slim, stunning genes, as Margaret did, and I was cool with that. I got the ability to ride a horse, and Margaret didn't. So, I spent many days doing just that. I hid from the nasty voice in my head that reminded me of my imperfections, and busied myself with riding, and nuzzling the horses and their soft manes. I was determined to be me, and not take on the brunt of jokes, so I distanced myself from my family and stayed around the horses – which also sadly showed up for my lack of friends.

The only place I was allowed to go was the riding club during the day, and to agricultural shows with my horse. But even then, I had to be back home in bed by evening. My father worked long hours and always supported whatever my mother said, so I knew there was no point in asking him for any leniency.

As for friends, the few I had seemed to think I was stuck up and rude. They were always quick to criticise me, and over time, I found myself distancing from them. It was hurtful to be judged in this way, but I didn't know how to change their perception of me. So instead, I kept to myself and focused on my passion for horses, finding solace in their company and the peace of the countryside.

It was a lonely existence, but I held onto the hope that someday I would find true friends who would accept me for who I was. And until then, I had my horse and the beauty of the natural world to keep me company.

At the end of year nine, our family had moved 300 kilometres south to a very small country town. My father was a pharmacist, and he had bought the one in the town, supplying drugs and medicines to about 4000 people. The shop sat on the main street, with pale green tiles around the door frame and a set of tall, green scales out the front, which was chained to a block of cement. The scales were so heavy they came with the purchase of the business. There was a slot to put in your twenty cents so that you could weigh yourself. I loved watching people use the scales.

The glass door and windows displayed the latest perfumes, trinkets and goodies on sale. For the size of the community, it was a busy shop. My father prepared and dispensed the drugs and potions, whilst my mother looked after the front of the business. She did all the buying, the stock taking, customer service, and managing the staff. This meant they needed to work long hours, and they didn't have time to collect me and my sister from a local school. The small community didn't support a senior school, so we were shipped off to attend a boarding school in the city.

As a boarding school student, I quickly learned the harsh reality of being surrounded by privileged and entitled teenage girls. Being one of the new girls made me an easy target for their taunts and teasing. It wasn't just my unfashionable sack dresses that made me stand out, it was the way they treated me. My appearance, braids, and even the way my loose uniform fit became the subject of ridicule. I tried to keep my head down and study hard but despite my attempts to focus on my studies, I found it difficult to ignore the constant bullying. I was called names, intimidated, and even coerced into giving up my pocket money and personal belongings like lipstick and perfume that my father had given me from his pharmacy. The bullying began on my first day and persisted until my last. Though I felt powerless against their cruel behaviour, I refused to show weakness and instead became stronger because of it.

I completed my school at year twelve, but I wasn't happy in those last two years at school. My body had grown, and I wanted to let the world know about it. I wanted my unrestrained curls to flow free, but I conformed to the rules that were set upon me by the school and braided it back against my head. My sack-like uniform left everything to the imagination, it was huge and showed nothing of my 'new' body. When we visited the uniform shop, my Mum had insisted on buying one size too big saying, "You'll grow into it." The uniform was scratchy and swivelled around my body like a sack. My chest filled my new bra, and yet no one knew. I wanted to share the news, just like so many others in my year.

Accusations came in many forms and one day I was asked to present to the headmistress' office. As I sat there, my mind raced with confusion and disbelief. She accused me of being pregnant, just because of a rumour she had heard about one of the year 12 girls. I was taken aback and couldn't find the words to defend myself. This wasn't the first time I was wrongly accused of things I didn't do. I had been called a "slut" so many times, even though I was still a virgin. It was as if people assumed it was me who had done it, even before being questioned.

Walking away from the boarding school on my final day, I felt a wave of relief wash over me. I was free from the constant torment of the other girls. They teased me for everything, from my clothes to my looks. They called me names, intimidated me, and even stole from me. But no more. As I left, I felt the tension in my shoulders begin to ease and the strain in my neck gradually loosened. Finally, I was away from the toxic environment of the boarding school and its nasty inhabitants.

Mum had been asking me what I wanted to do, but to be honest I had no idea about any role that was meant for me. Back at school in the boarding house common room on Sunday nights when we all came in to watch 60 Minutes, the latest current affair program, we'd discuss possible various roles, jobs and future studies for each of us. I recall I was never very keen on anything that anyone suggested, and just added my ideas, rather than taking anything away from the conversations. The girls were all so prickly that one wrong comment could cause weeks of angst.

I shuddered as the memory of these times came to me.

I considered my options. I could work in 'the shop', my father's pharmacy, for a year if he'd have me. I could leave and head to Perth and find a job, I could go travelling… the ideas started to flow fast. I made a mental note to discuss my situation with my mother and father later that day.

As I strolled around the house, trying to reacquaint myself with the surroundings, I came to a sudden realisation. I had never tasted the sweet freedom of being myself, of 'not giving a damn', and living my life unburdened by the opinions of others. My entire life had been about pleasing those around me, with my mother always reminding me to consider what the neighbours would think. And then there was my sister, the star of the family, interning at a prestigious hospital in Perth. I had always lived in her shadow, never quite measuring up. But now, I was determined to break free from these chains and discover who I truly am.

It had been impressed upon me for years to be who everyone expected me to be. I had no idea who that person was, but I'd tried hard to fit in. Then when I attended school, we were kept on a strict doctrine of what activities we could do. So this meant there was never any room for finding out who I actually was. Let alone what I wanted to do. I had no idea. Now that I had thought about it, it was stifling. My self-esteem, which seemed to be normal before I went to boarding school, had received a battering and I now had fears that I had never felt before.

Rather than talking to my parents straight away I wanted to weigh up everything and decided I would talk to an older friend in town who had travelled before she got married. I wanted to find out what it was like to go to Europe, and what she had gained from it. Back some ten years ago she had travelled around by herself, even when the act of solo travel was considered very risky business. We met for a coffee and chatted about her experience. She showed me her photo album and we laughed as we looked at the scenes and she shared her story. She said it was transformational for her, and it certainly sounded that way. Even so, as I walked down the steps from her house, I decided it wasn't the right time for me to travel just yet. So, I would find some work in the country town and try to discover some of my chutzpah again. I walked towards the shop to see mum and dad and tell them my news.

Living in a small town had its pros and cons, and one of them was the fact that everyone knew each other's business. My parents ran a local shop, which meant they were always in the know. Mum would often come home with the latest gossip about who was doing what, who was in trouble, and who was pregnant. Dad, on the other hand, was content to stay behind the counter, hidden from view. Mum was the outgoing one, always up for a party or a game of tennis. This meant that whatever I did was instantly broadcast across the town's rumour mill. Walking down the street, I was greeted with comments and whispers from the ladies who knew all my business. It was suffocating, and I longed for a bit of privacy.

"Aw, aren't you looking good today dear?" a lady with white hair said as she smiled up at me.

"Thank you," I replied, smiling back at her, not quite sure who she was.

"I heard from Gloria Lance that you were seen with that Fisher boy, dear. What's happening there, I thought you were with Edward?" the lady replied.

"Um, no, well, yes I am and no," I stammered. This town was unbelievable! One night out with someone and they think you're getting married.

I kept my head down and walked down the hill to where the shop front was. Opening the door, I was greeted by an older gentleman holding the drugs in a pharmacy guild paper bag in his left hand. In his right hand was his walking stick. I loved to talk to the over 70's, they always seemed to have so much to share.

I opened the door wide to let him out. "There you go." I liked this man. "Mind the step there," I said with a smile as he stepped down the single step and out onto the pavement.

Often, they would then stop and have a chat, and then be on their way. This time however, he shuffled off grunting something that sounded like 'haroo', not looking me in the eye. I closed the door and walked inside.

The small-town gossip and comments were endless, so I tried very hard to keep my head down and stay out of trouble. Just like in boarding school. Yet, the questions kept coming.

"What are you going to do with your life?" the local accountant asked as I delivered some drugs to his shop.

"I heard you are with that Edward bloke, Ron Smith's boy from Jingalup way, is that true?" Another asked as I waited in line at the local IGA.

I smiled and nodded, but didn't offer anything in return. Instead, I deflected and asked him about his lambs and how they were getting along. It was a safe bet as farmers all had lambs appearing at this time of year! Even though I had no clue as to who he was, he chatted away the whole time about lambs until we were served.

It was true, I had been seeing a man named Edward, a farmer who lived just outside of town. He had a nice look, with dark brown hair and eyes to match. Edward drove a bright yellow Toyota FJ Cruiser, which I thought was a bit odd, but it suited him. We had started to develop a connection during my final years of school, and I had even invited him to be my date for the school ball. It was a low-key affair, and I didn't want anyone to pry into my personal life. At the time, I thought he was everything I was looking for. He owned a sheep and wheat farm where he lived with his elderly mother. The undulating land had great paddocks and facilities, with plenty of space for me to keep my horses. To me, he was the perfect catch.

When I had time off, I would work on the farm with Edward. The work on the farm varied. Sometimes we would repair stockyards or fences, other times we'd drive around checking fences, dams, troughs and stock.

When the job was done Edward would step back and review the work we'd done together, "Well, it's good enough for a sheep and wheat farm," he'd say as he rocked back on his heels.

I knew Edward's mother was pretty much a recluse, so I tried to keep my distance. She never showed her face when I entered the house. She was a good cook though, as I'd sampled many of her scones, fruit cake and jam tarts when we had the shearers in and she was preparing their food. Only then did I get the taste of her delights, and they certainly hit the mark. In the months we spent together I never was invited into the house, not even for dinner; however Edward did come to our place many times. I lived with Mum and Dad not far down the road, so it was easy for him to come to us. For that reason and the fact that I would never have been given permission, I never stayed the night at his place. I didn't need to ask. I knew the word Mum would say "What, stay at his house? There is no way that will happen whilst you're living under our roof."

The days we spent together were filled with dust, sheep and the smell of lanolin from the wool. I loved the freedom and the evenings when the distant hills glowed golden, as the sun headed west to set across the distant ocean off the west Australia coast. As much as I loved the country, I missed the ocean and always felt the distance from it.

The sun was shining and the gentle breeze blew my black curls into my face, as I swatted a fly. My pony was wandering up the paddock behind a mob of sheep. Their faint smell of lanolin reaching my nostrils, along with the eucalyptus from the tall trees surrounding us as I ambled along. As a rider on a pony, I was wandering aimlessly behind them, hoping I knew the paddock well enough to bring them to the correct gate. We rounded a hill I could see the ute parked up ahead at a gateway, so I knew I was bringing them to the correct paddock. I'd been on my pony for over an hour now, and the vastness of these paddocks and the exact location of gates always baffled me. A fly buzzed, and I swiped it before it could land on my nose and work its way into my nostrils. My pony was a show jumper, and she usually just knew fast. Fast and strong was her normal, she was brave and jumped huge heights. So to have her ambling along was a welcome change for her training and sanity.

We'd done some miles, this pony and I. She'd been a station mare when my parents found her for me. I had been craving my next pony that would take me somewhere, and they sourced this charismatic, opinionated mare. She was black as the ace of spades, sure footed, and sprightly. She could jump double her height and often won ribbons for speed, showing off her ability to jump, spin and jump again. When I was completing and came back from my round Mum would say to me "I couldn't watch you, I was so worried. Those jumps are huge."

I'm not sure why she came, she was always so nervous when we competed. My pony was my equal in age, and as I left school, I knew it was time to retire her from competitions. She had been with me since I was nine, and we had won many ribbons along the way. The little black pony, and the girl with the black curly hair. As I grew older, and we advanced in the rankings, we became one of the top junior riders in the state. I often jumped at the Perth Royal Show, feeling the excitement of being in the middle of the city and being able to ride my horse. Friends from all walks of life came to watch me ride when we were there. It was a huge thrill, especially when we brought home ribbons.

Even though I no longer competed with her, just riding behind sheep across the hills was good for her ageing muscles, so I loved the fact she was still being useful. Plus, she was a solid character who I knew and loved. I knew her quirks, and the way her rhythmic footfalls on the ground went. I knew which buttons to push to ask her to act, and how to calm her down when needed. Having left school and recently feeling out of sorts with the world, she was a constant that kept me going. The feel of her underneath me was supportive.

Suddenly she gave a jolt, and I looked up to see what had alerted her. She had spotted a couple of crows in the distance, and Edward's dogs running around excited. Must get on with the sheep herding, I thought.

Edward put up with me having a horse, even though he'd never had them on the farm before. The first time I mustered the sheep, I loved it. It was hard work and bloody hot, but so exciting. My heart raced from the exhilaration, and from the way my pony mare worked the sheep. She was a natural. Edward taught me a lot about moving sheep and the positions on the mob. Initially, I was reluctant to chase any escapees as I had so much to learn. Everything was new to me. Then I got the hang of it as I practiced moving them around.

Now I loved the sensation of bringing them in, that sudden speed and then stopping to rest the animals. My pony was good at closing gates as I sat on her, and this skill was used often when bringing in the sheep. Occasionally, I'd not even bother with opening the gate, instead opting to jump the strainer post or gate if I needed to get into a paddock by myself. I'd canter my pony up to the fence and she'd fly over it, just like she would in an arena.

The windmill creaked into action as we neared the bend that took us down to the yards, and I felt the gentle breeze on my face. The flies had been in my eyes for hours, I was over them! Finally, I was nearly there. I dropped the branch and leaves I had broken from a tree that I'd been using to swish away the flies. The ute appeared beside me, and Edward gave me instructions on where they needed to go. He'd been and closed the last gates behind us, and now had set the yards ready for them to enter.

I was in the midst of herding sheep when one of them broke out of the line. With a sense of belonging on the land, I trotted over to bring her back in. But then another ewe broke out on the other side and the ute was too far away to help. So, I asked my pony to spin and gallop, and she willingly obliged. Gosh this was good! It was an exhilarating feeling to block and canter around, moving my pony from side to side to prevent any further escapes.

I could see the gate we needed to get them in, yet it seemed the sheep were doing everything they could to avoid going in. That's odd I thought, these ewes should know where they are going. Maybe it was the horse, so I hung back to allow them to settle.

Edward came around the side with the ute, with his trusty dogs. I stood and watched as he helped the sheep and ewe into their confines with finesse and precision. The gates shut and with the sheep safely away, we were done.

This was why I loved this place. Exhilarated, tired and dusty I got off and walked my pony putting her into a yard away from the ewes and began to unsaddle her. Brushing her down to remove the sweat and dirt from where it formed under the saddle, I thanked her for a job well done. Making sure the trough was full and clean, I threw her some hay and walked into the shed.

Looking up at me and holding the broom where he had been sweeping the wool remnants off the floorboards, Edward said. 'Well done, great ride?'

'Yeah, it's beautiful out there. I love this place,' I replied waving my hands out to the paddocks.

"We'll leave the sheep here overnight so that they settle, and then we can start early tomorrow drenching and tagging them," Edward said.

'Cool, what's next?' I asked. He didn't answer immediately, just frowned so I continued, "We could go to the pub, it is Sunday night, and the session will be in full swing."

Edward's eyes crinkled, 'Fancy swimming in the big dam?' He said with a sly grin spreading across his face.

'Maybe....' I knew that look.

He doesn't want to go to the pub with other sweaty, drunk bodies; he wants to be alone. Alone with me.

'OK. I have a bit of work to do to clean up, you go, and I'll be there in a bit. Give me maybe thirty minutes, is that ok?' he asked.

'Sure is, I'll see you inside" I replied walking into the house, to clean and wash. I knew that grin on his face, he wanted to have some intimate time together.

It wasn't until I had left school that we slept together. I wanted to go to some riding event up in Perth, and Mum couldn't take me. So, as he had a car (that yellow Cruiser) that could tow the horse float, we planned a date weekend. We would stay with my riding friend Georgia, where my horse could be stabled at her place, and we could stay in her spare room. She was a bit older than me, and she had been telling me tales of sex for years, and I knew this was the right time. It was perfect.

The word 'virgin' had been bandied around my boarding school for years. It always seemed to be loaded with so much when the other girls talked about it. I felt there was so much pressure placed on each other on 'losing it'. It seemed we all wanted to gain that sexual experience, so we could say we had. I'd heard many stories from the girls, and whilst it was intriguing to me, it wasn't high on my priorities.

Sometimes I would pretend I knew what they were talking about, just to fit in, but I really had no idea.

Working up to the day was huge. I was lucky I had other things on my mind to take my focus away from what was expected of me later that evening. This was a major milestone for me. I thought Edward and I were very much in love and we had been talking about taking this next step in our relationship for a long time, but we could never find the right place or time to be alone. He had already had sex before but was very patient and put up with my wild insecurities, and my fear of parents finding out. I wanted to, but then I didn't, then I would be sad that I didn't and annoyed that I was teasing him. I seemed to be all over the place. All of this meant Edward might not put up with me for much longer if I didn't succumb. So there was some insecurity in me that said I had to do "it".

That night finally came and as I lay on the bed in Georgia's pink childhood bedroom, I felt very awkward and sort of waiting for something to happen. We sat on the bed. He smelt of baby powder as he'd just come from the shower. I closed my eyes and kissed him, it was warm and inviting, distracting me from the thoughts that were looming. I concentrated on his kiss, and the feel of his body so close. Suddenly, I was really enjoying the experience, and knew it was time. I said, "let's do it".

Silently he went to get his condoms and as I sat there on the bed waiting for him, I had these mixed emotions. "Here I go. This is it" I thought. I was happy that I was finally going to experience this milestone, yet it really scared me, I could feel it in my gut that it might not be good. I felt he really loved me and respected me, but the thoughts kept coming...I could get pregnant or something. I also felt, in a way, that I was letting down my family. So often I'd heard that premarital sex was taboo. By the time he came back from getting his condoms, I was letting my fears get the best of me, and I no longer was in the mood.

The pink eiderdown was inviting and I lay down along it as he joined me side by side. We started to talk about life, it's ups and downs, and things he had never shared. I felt so happy to be included in his life. I turned to look at his face and could see he was struggling as well. We talked some more and then I got distracted as he kissed me tenderly. The passion increased and at some point, he asked me, "Are you sure?" I realised it was exactly what I wanted and I wouldn't want it with anyone else.

We undressed each other and got in bed together, continuing to make out. The act itself was a bit clumsy and was very painful. But because we had such a comfortable relationship, I was able to communicate with him how it was hurtful and he offered to go slow or even stop, but I told him it was fine. I truly wanted to go ahead with it. Of course, he went slowly for me.

After that I got up and went to the toilet, expecting some bleeding, and as I walked down the hallway, I ran into Georgia's mum. She smiled, but didn't say anything, I pointed to the bathroom and rushed on. Awkward!

In the bathroom, I saw my face in the mirror and said to my reflection, "That was weird". Leaving the cubicle, I looked again at my reflection, "I sure hope it gets better than that" as I walked out the door and back down the hallway.

Our relationship lasted for about two years in all. The adults in my life thought he was just a fling, not someone to spend the rest of my life with. I felt pressured to show them they were wrong. It took me a while to realise that I was chasing a dream, and not the man himself. I didn't want to settle down, get married, and have children. Who was I kidding? That was a dream for someone else.

I wanted adventure, and fun. I wanted to find out who I was, and what made me excited. I had a bucket list of ever lengthening desires to tick off. In the time being at home and working in the shop, I had grown, and found something of myself again. I wanted to explore, to share my dreams, my thoughts, and find out what else.

I wanted to be the girl who partied with everyone else, and drink as much as they did. I wanted to enjoy life and it was exhausting doing that when living at home. I always felt I was watching my back for what my mother and her gossips would be saying next.

It remained that whilst I was at home, I didn't have any close friends, no one at school had really made a mark on me, and for my mother, no one in town was suitable for her daughter. Other girls from farms in the district had also been away at school, different ones, and occasionally we met up, but no one considered me their bestie. Having moved to the town only two years prior, I was definitely not a local. And having left good friends behind where we used to live, I found myself becoming a loner, someone who read books, listened to loud music when I could, and someone who loved horses.

I joined the local swimming club, and that along with training sessions gave me a purpose and some new friends. We would train twice a week, in the outdoor town pool, and compete on weekends when I wasn't riding. Mostly the events were in other local towns, so there always was a minimum two-hour drive to get to the pool. I loved the team we created, and how we cheered each other on. It became very addictive to be part of that community.

Up until now there had been so many rules in my life, rules that I know were there to protect me, yet they actually stifled me. Rules that stifled everything out of my creativity, told me what to do, how and when to do it. I had learnt the hard way by pushing boundaries, and felt the consequences that arose if I didn't obey.

My parents were well-off, even considered to be wealthy. But living a wealthy life was not always the answer; maybe I could find that as I travelled in the urban, poor and mixed race places that the world has to offer. I didn't truly know who I was, I was just a girl who did what I was told. It was time for me to spread my wings, so I decided to go and travel to the UK, a place that seemed a world away from the farm and rural landscape as I knew it. A place that might share with me some answers, some ideas, and some fun times.

On the inside, I had grown rebellious and just wanted to do my own thing. I wouldn't be told what to "do" with MY life anymore! Those so-called responsible adults had shown me they still had lots to learn. So at the age of sixteen, nearly seventeen, I went travelling around the world. My limited friends were strapped for cash, or had other priorities, so I packed my backpack, bought myself a Lonely Planet and booked my flight for a solo adventure. I left my pony with my family and headed off. I'm not sure what I wanted to achieve, it was just the feeling of getting away and doing my own thing that attracted me.

As I stepped through customs, I left my parents sobbing in the hall. It must have been contagious because as I turned to wave goodbye the tears streamed down my own cheeks. They didn't last long though as I walked into the customs hall and realised I was starting my new adventure. I flew through the air for the next 24 hours and was very excited thinking about what lay ahead. The thrill of somewhere new, somewhere that no one knew me was amazing. Away from that small town, and small mentality. I was free and I could indulge my every whim. I could find opportunities for self-reflection, for self-discovery and to make new friends. I had a bucket list to tick off.

Arriving in the UK, I quickly found myself work, and made new friends. It was freedom and excitement all wrapped into one. I was keen to really experience life with new people, and so I went out as often as I could. I found myself work as a live-in nanny for one of the top eventing riders based out on their farm near Stonehenge. The hours were long, and the work was so totally different to anything else I'd done in my life to that point, yet it was a super experience. It was here that I realised whilst I could stay on a horse, and ask it to jump fences, I wasn't really a "good" rider. I was a "bush hack", I could stick in the saddle when the horse got a bit bumpy, but I wasn't tall and elegant, like so many of the English riders. I didn't look like those amazing tall long-legged riders who make the art of riding look effortless. I also didn't have endless money to spend on trivial items for my horse to make it "look good". No, I was someone who got it done, and did it simply. Yet the voice in my head was constantly telling me to "give it up Amanda - you're no good, they're laughing at you". This image, the constant negative voices in my head and the preciseness of riding in the UK and grooming your horse for hours made me give it up. I decided to concentrate on being a great children's nanny instead. Riding was something I could do when I returned back to Western Australia, and in the safety of my home town.

TOM

To love someone is to love yourself.
To be in a relationship is to understand more about you.
True love comes in many shapes and sizes.

I met Tom whilst travelling in Thailand. I had been on a bender on a beach in Koh Samui. I'd travelled there with a girlfriend, who, let's say, I hadn't been getting along with. We'd met whilst I was working in the UK, and I thought as we could work together, we also could travel together. But it wasn't working. I'd really tried to put up with her strange ways; truly, I had tried. For days we had been together and I'd had to bite my lip, and not say anything.

One day when we decided to try out magic mushrooms, I told her the truth about how I felt and two days later I was alone. Initially it was great, I loved the peace, and my own company. The backpacker's resort which I was camped in was really a stylish hideaway situated on the west coast of Koh Samui.

The resort consisted of seventy little huts made from bamboo. They all faced the ocean, had use of a pool and came with a camp breakfast. All for a couple of US dollars. In the vicinity, there were various services provided by enterprising locals if you wanted to pamper yourself. These services included purifying facials, aromatic salt scrubs, and ancient Thai massages, all of which were carried out in the open air in this amazing resort. The resort was bustling with travellers from all over the world, including couples, singles, best friends, and even strangers from different parts of Australia. There were plenty of visitors from New Zealand, South Africa, England, America, Canada, Mexico, numerous European countries- from virtually every corner of the globe.

It was an interesting environment, and a place for me to get my act together. I spent my time alone swimming, drinking with the other backpackers, sharing mushrooms, and setting my world straight. I was trying to act like a grown-up, or maybe I was avoiding the fact that I had to return home and actually be a grown-up. I was acting like someone who did not have a care in the world, and had all the time and money to enjoy it. The problem was that money was running out. Since leaving home I had managed to eke out my dollars by finding work, and then travelling, but the funds were drying up. I needed work, and that meant I needed to get a grip on myself and act like an adult.

One morning, whilst recovering from a huge night, I decided to go down to the beach to try to walk and swim away my hangover. My bikini was constantly on whilst I'd been on the island, so I threw on my shorts and a T-shirt and started the short walk down to the beach. This part of the beach was filled with monolithic rocks, and secluded coves. I loved it and always felt safe. As I walked, picking up shells and skimming them across the water I got thinking about the next part of my life. During my stay in the UK, I'd taken office work in London, and had gathered some useful skills, including being a supervisor in a large call centre. If I went back to the UK I knew I could go back to that company, and they would probably take me back, and they paid well too. Or, now that I was down in the southern hemisphere, I could head back to Perth and do something there.

But did I want to go back home? Was it time? Had I seriously had enough of partying and was it truly time to make a go of my life? As these thoughts swirled in my head I rounded the next corner of the cove to what was known as the elephant rock.

There, over by the big elephant looking rocks, was a European looking man. Nothing unusual about that, that's where we were, on an isolated island full of backpackers. He was sitting in a meditation type pose, and it appeared he hadn't noticed me. I kept walking, thinking I wanted to continue contemplating my future. But as I walked past, I felt his eyes on me and all thoughts of my future fell away into oblivion, refusing to resurface. I looked back to see if he was watching, and sure enough he was smiling at me. Actually smiling at me! His sun bleached blonde hair was twisted in ratty tails, looking like it needed a good wash and comb…or maybe a cut. A ratty-haired god I thought, as I continued walking. "Maybe he has the answer to my questions." As I continued walking, I felt my breathing speed up, and excitement building from somewhere deep within me. I kept walking, feet splashing the clear blue ocean water, trying to calm my racing heart, and leaving footprints in the golden beach sand. I don't know why, but I wanted to run. It was like a bogeyman was chasing me. I controlled my urge and kept walking.

I turned back again and he was still there by the rock, sitting in the same pose. Yet, I couldn't stop this mad feeling of butterflies in my stomach. What was it? In the end, I stripped off my clothes and dived into the ocean to clear my head. I swam deep and looked at the corals and fish as they swam past. I held my breath as I swam peacefully under the water. As I came up for air I turned and lay on my back, allowing the sun to gently warm and brown my body as I floated across the ocean swell. I was there for a long time, and didn't want to come out. By the time I did, he was gone, and so was my hangover.

I walked back to my hut and didn't see anyone, so I ventured to the breakfast shack. Thankfully, no one was there either, other than the Thai cook. Deciding the blond god was a mirage and a result of my hangover, I packed my bag for a day of adventure. I hopped on my scooter to go around the island and get some treats. The only traffic on the island were the tourist coaches taking people to the expensive resorts, and travellers on their scooters. A couple of hours in, I pulled into what could be called a bus shelter. I'm not sure of its purpose, but it was a great place to stop and cool down from the hot midday heat. When packing my bags I had forgotten to refill my water bottle and it was now hot and nearly empty. I needed to be careful, so I took just a few sips. Unpacking my towel, I placed it across a wooden table under the shelter and lay down. Closing my eyes to get some rest, I lay there peacefully for what seemed like thirty minutes. Then I heard footsteps.

My eyes flew open. As a lone female traveller in a foreign country, I had to be careful. I'd heard too many stories from fellow travellers, ones that didn't end well. Ones that mostly involved locals trying their luck on unsuspecting and innocent travellers. I reached for my towel and wrapped it around me, to stop whoever it was from looking at my body. Sitting up on the table I heard a familiar accent ask, "Can I share some space?"

I looked up into the brown eyes of the blonde god on the beach.

Stuttering, I replied, "y... y... yes ok" and moved over.

"I'm Tom, by the way." he said in a soft Australian accent.

"yaah, um. Hi."

Keeping my gaze firmly on the palm tree across the path so my feelings wouldn't show on my face, I reluctantly gave him my name, "Amanda".

Over the next few hours, having shared his water and some crisps, I found out that he had a quirky habit of bouncing his leg when he was thinking, and he had come over to Thailand to recover from a nasty relationship breakup. He'd been here for just over two weeks, and on the island just a few days. That explained why I had not seen him around before. He'd been keeping quiet, he said, and didn't want to get involved with anyone. He was heading back to Perth – yes Perth, my home town - in just under a week. In those few hours we had talked, really talked, laughed, shared stories of travelling, and generally enjoyed each other's company. This person sitting inches away from me, bouncing his leg up and down, was talking to me and I was having fun. My stomach was in knots, yet I felt comfortable, so what was with that? I pondered. I wasn't looking for a boyfriend at the time; they would just get in the way. But I could tell that this sweating, breathing stranger was interested in me.

"I'm not looking for another relationship in the immediate future," he said sometime later. I played that over and over in my head as I finally took the scooter back to my hut. I thought that was the end of it.

Yet, as fate would have it, we did see each other again on the island, a few days later. The tension from the previous meetings seemed to have gone, and we managed to keep it simple. Over the next few days, we chatted and hung out together having fun. That was it. But we got on well, and that to me was a huge bonus. During our time together we discussed what I was doing, and my questions about where to go next. He was level headed and helped me see both sides - heading back to the UK or heading home. The final decision was mine, but he certainly assisted me with the choice.

Then the day came when Tom needed to head back to the mainland as he had booked tickets from Bangkok to Kathmandu in Nepal. He wanted to experience the Himalayan mountain peaks, some Buddhism and one of the world's most fascinating cities.

The day he was to depart I walked with him down to the ferry piers to catch the two hour High-Speed Catamaran to Koh Phangan. From there he would take the twelve plus hour bus ride from Surat Thani back to Bangkok. We hugged just before he boarded the ferry and I felt a tear in my eye. He was a fabulous person, and I was sad to be saying goodbye. Yet, I knew he had a couple more weeks of fun and adventure ahead of him. We had exchanged email addresses, but no promises were made.

AUSTRALIA

*The most blissful country on earth.
Hardened by age, and sun and drenched by rain.
It's diversity is its beauty, which
Brings life to so many.*

Within days of Tom's departure I knew it was time to go, and decided I needed to return to being a business person back in Perth. I needed to get a job, a house and all of those things about being an adult. Once I'd made that decision I knew it was right, and booked myself onto my flight home.

Coming back to Perth was a huge shock to me. It was so small compared to London, and so lacking in quirky cafes, cool history and heritage architecture, or weekend flea markets and delightful boutiques. Never one to stay negative for long, I shifted my focus to the positive aspects of the situation and convinced myself that what I loved about Perth is its openness, gorgeous bright sunny days, and stunning beaches. This in itself made me grateful, plus the fact it was closer to Mum and Dad and to family. Another plus was I knew the streets and which beaches to go to. My travels had brought about a huge sense of wellbeing in me, and I knew I could master most things, even though they were only small things.

Mum and Dad still lived in the country and so there was no opportunity to go back and live with them. Instead, I found myself a place to stay that was close to both the beach and the city, and then found work really quickly. The girl I shared accommodation with was constantly out and busy with a huge circle of friends. Whilst I could have tagged along with her, I chose not to. Since I didn't have any acquaintances who piqued my interest, I realised that I needed to find a way to get involved with like-minded individuals. I knew that Australians loved their sports, so I decided to renew my diving certifications. My rationale was that it might help me forge new connections and maybe join a group or club. I wasn't entirely certain, but the plan seemed feasible to me.

Even though I knew tall, blonde, suntanned and handsome Tom had come back to Perth, and I had his contact details, I didn't want to contact him. Who knew if those feelings we had back in Koh Samui, that seemed a lifetime ago now, would remain? I didn't want to take the chance that maybe it was just a fling. A holiday romance. We certainly had some fun, got drunk in smoky bars together, shared confessions and passions and dreams for our future life together. It was intoxicating whilst we were there, but would that be the same when we are back in a job, dating and meeting parents?

I've heard all about these holiday romances that never work. People go away and with the help of alcohol or other drugs they have the confidence to make a move on someone who isn't their typical type of person. They think at the time it is a good thing, and they are in love. But really, is it infatuation? When they get back home they realise that the person they fell for isn't actually as good looking or as charming as they initially thought. I had resisted searching for him on social media, I didn't want to know whether he was with someone else, or he'd moved on. Some well-meaning girlfriends had said to me, just connect with him and see what happens… I knew it was so easy to reach out and reconnect…but I didn't want to.

I was reluctant to find out if it was just the magic of being somewhere new, meeting someone new, and being able to be me, as nobody else knew me. My reticence to experience normality, or even boredom together was stopping me from doing anything. I did know for certain that it wasn't about the sex, because there had been none.

The fear of real life had taken hold. I was back, I was in a working life again, but I still didn't want to know what Tom was like after a long day at work, or to have dinner conversations at a quiet kitchen table in a flat in the suburbs. I wanted to remember that magic as it was and not find out I was just making it up in my head. I wanted to cherish my dreams and not break the bubble, be swept up by it, be thrilled by it, be seduced by it, and ride it out for as long as it could possibly last.

I was still smarting from a London relationship. Not from Edward, though. I'd gotten over that liaison well and truly and had moved on. This time, I'd met someone in London and thought I was in love, and then after a few months of dating I was ghosted.

It was excruciating.

I was excited about this guy, I'd demonstrated interest, he'd responded, we had gone out over a period of months, we'd had sex a couple of times, and then nothing. Even though I thought we had a good thing going, when I sent texts, emails, tried calling, I got nothing back.

I tried to seek answers and then was met with silence from this guy.

I had no idea what had happened. I was clueless and my mind had started taking off on all sorts of trajectories. For a long time I hadn't been able to close that loop. I still hadn't been able to heal and I knew that there would be some time before I could actually open up to someone else and be treated the way I deserved.

So even though I'd come back to Perth, I was waiting. Waiting for the right time to make contact with Tom. Maybe it was because I wanted to sort out my living situation, so that I wasn't in a single bed in a tiny apartment. Or maybe I wanted to wait until my heart was healed. Either way, I didn't want to make contact.

I wanted to delay any love connections coming my way, and being single was more desirable to me than having a relationship that could result in further heartbreak.

To keep myself from going stir crazy I booked myself into a dive course the following weekend at a scuba shop not far up the coast. That way I could meet new people and have some fun, whilst diving - something I loved. The evening of the first session I walked into the course, having just come from work. Around the table was a group of people all from Water Corp, the state based supplier of water, waste-water & drainage services. They all seemed to know one another and were all interacting. Great I thought, so much for meeting people, they were only interested in themselves.

I found a seat away from the others and sat down, getting my pens and paper ready for my learning. As I sorted myself, I heard a voice beside me ask, "Is this seat taken?" I knew that voice. Looking up I gazed into those amazing deep brown eyes of Tom.

I felt my heart skip a beat. "Whoa" I mouthed smiling; in fact, I reckon I was beaming.

His blonde hair gleamed as he stretched down to place his bag on the table. His thin, blue T-Shirt lifted a fraction to show a flat, almost ripped stomach. I swallowed hard.

"Hey, what are you doing here?" he said as he pulled the seat out and put his tattered canvas bag on the floor.

"No, wait, what are you doing here? Last time I heard you were headed to Kathmandu," I stammered, my voice a tad too loud at the relief of seeing him again.

"I'm upgrading my qualifications, and you?" he shrugged and then added "Are you all OK?"

Was he asking because I looked different? I tugged at my work shirt, and touched my hair. "I'm fine, thanks." I looked away trying to figure out what was going on. I could feel the heat rising in my cheeks. God Amanda, why can't you get your act together?"

The instructor walked in, and all went silent. My heart pumped hard, it was Tom, and he looked as gorgeous as ever. He still had that gorgeous sun bleached blonde hair, his T shirt rippled under his muscles, and he was just so, so serene.

I felt all gooey. Amanda, what are you doing, I asked myself. You don't need a man in your life, not this man, or any man. Stop those thoughts right there, I heard a voice in my head say, as I heard another voice saying "just try and stop me"

The first part of the course was first aid, and needless to say we partnered up. I had just come from work, and still had my make up on, and bright red lipstick. When it came time to do our CPR on the dummies I jumped in first, complete with my red lipstick. When I came back up I had smeared it across the dummy and my face! The room roared with laughter as I looked around and realised what I'd done.

I rolled my eyes. What an embarrassment. Right in front of Tom!

I looked around for a sachet of steriliser to wipe it off, thinking that should be safety 101, having something to sterilise the dummies after they were used. There was nothing around, so I walked out to find something. By the time I came back into the room, Tom was chatting animatedly to another guy.

I sat down at my desk, and completed my theory questions, listening to the guys laughing and joking together. Was I jealous? Maybe.

Finally, when we had a break we got to stand next to one another at the coffee bar.

'I didn't know you dived,' I said, stuffing a biscuit in my mouth. I was starving because I'd been late leaving work and didn't have time to grab anything to eat. Plus, I was still on a limited budget so it was biscuits for dinner tonight.

'You right there?' he said laughing as crumbs scattered down my shirt.

Oh god I thought, I'm making such a fool of myself. "Um yeah, bit hungry, sorry" I replied, brushing down my shirt. Concentrate Amanda! I chided myself.

"Yes I dive," he said in response to my earlier question. "In fact I'm learning to become an instructor and need to attend this class as the first step. What about you, is this something you've always done?"

I suppressed a smile as I carried the first aid equipment to the next table. "Yes, I learned whilst travelling, and I've dived in some pretty cool places since then. I'm here to upgrade and meet new people – you know as they say at PADI (Professional Association of Diving Instructors) – go places, meet people, and do things," I said looking down away from those eyes.

He laughed and as I looked up I saw his smile reaching his eyes, "Have you met anyone yet?" he asked

"Not really," I lied grinning.

"How was Kathmandu?" I asked, changing the subject.

"Fantastic, I loved the meditation, it really got me thinking about my life," he replied as the instructor walked over to us and asked us to sit down.

The course continued the following evening, and then we dived for the next three weekends. Over the time we got talking and actually managed a coffee after one dive and a beer after another. It was enjoyable, but I wasn't prepared to move into any form of serious relationship; friendship was enough. There was a wonderful marina just up from the dive shop, filled with designer shops, a brewery, patisserie and trendy coffee bars. We frequented the marina and all it offered, trying various taste sensations, ice-creams and beers after our dives.

Even though I was determined to be "just friends" this guy was amazing. He had already shared with me stories of how he had spent many months under a psychologist following his toxic relationship break up, and sorting out who he was. This meant he was open to conversations, emotionally available and capable of listening to me. His laugh was infectious, he made me smile often, and he was fun to be around. He had shared his flaws, and his toxic break up had somehow made him vulnerable, which made me want him more. I wasn't falling for him and his charms though. I put up barriers and tried to kid myself he wasn't for me.

He was smart, and could see when I was kidding myself. He could see right through me and my protective measures. He made noises about me having some underlying issue, which I ignored.

"What is wrong with just seeing each other for coffee or a beer?" I spat back to his comment about my issue over a beer one night.

"I thought you might want something more." he said

"Leave it Tom, I'm not ready for this conversation" I said and promptly closed the debate, moving onto something diving related.

For the next few weeks we continued diving together, sharing coffees and beers. That was it.

Then late in summer he rang me at work and asked me out on a date.

"A date?" I asked

"Yes, I'm sick of this namby pamby thing we have going on. We're either here for the long haul or not. I can't just keep doing coffee!" he replied. He wanted to create a healthy loving relationship that would go the distance, with a solid base. His priority was to feel secure.

"Are you in or not?" he asked.

"Gosh, ok, I think so." I replied weakly. We arranged to meet that night for our 'date'.

That date was the turning point from us being just good friends to becoming a couple. Over the next few months we couldn't be separated, and started to explore our commitment to each other. We agreed we wanted to be together; however, we were actually not moving forward. He made me feel strong, and sexy and on top of the world. Yet something was wrong. We weren't going to that ultimate destination of a long term relationship. We skipped around moving in together and I knew that there was an issue. I suspected the problem was me. I didn't want to waste time, so I started to look at myself. Was I settling for less than I deserved, or what was possible for me? I don't think Tom was the issue. As hard as it was for me to accept, I really believed the issue was me.

My sense of what is possible was confused.

I needed to stop and get really clear on what I wanted.

The next morning after my coffee, I grabbed my journal, threw a towel over my shoulder and took off to the beach. It was a short walk, and the day was still young, so luckily "the Fremantle Doctor" the cooling onshore wind had not come in. The path to the beach from the apartment took me to a dog beach, and sometimes that was a bit stinky. To put it mildly the dog faeces stunk, and if I was going to be sitting here writing in my journal, I needed to be well away from that. I turned right as I got to the sand dunes and headed to a pleasant cove that faced south. Walking on the white pristine sands of the idyllic beach with its aquamarine water reminded me I really had heaven at my doorstep. All the places I had visited had nothing on this place. They might have the history, and the architecture, but nothing reached the beauty of the alluring Western Australian coastline. I found a space to sit on the sand, and rest myself against some rocks. The cove was very quiet and I was sharing it with only a handful of other people looking to cool off. The beauty of the WA coast and white sandy beaches was due to the sandstone that weathers to produce fine, frosted quartz sand grains. Interestingly, the sands made from shell or coral fragments just aren't as white.

Using a journal allowed me to write and just let the words flow without thinking too much about what I wrote. It didn't matter what I wrote, just as it came I would put words on paper. Then after I was done I would spend time reflecting back upon what I had written. If there were patterns to find, I'd usually find them through this process. It had worked many times before for me, so I had to give it a go this time. After sitting for over an hour pouring my heart into my journal I put my pen down and stopped. I rolled my shoulders, and shook my hand as I had become tight from writing so much. Reading what I'd written and looking into the patterns with relationships I could see I had been settling for less than what I deserved. I realised that I have chosen people in the past who have been unavailable, and I've covered it up with work, or travel. I made excuses for them, and for my lack of belief in myself. This was a shock and a challenge for me to realise. I could see now that I wasn't being loved and cherished in ways that I truly wanted.

The only way this pattern could stop was if I took responsibility and put in place steps to change. Once I realised this I started to be real about who I am, where I'd come from, and where I was going. There was stuff I'd hidden deep down, and wouldn't acknowledge. My belief was that at this age I should be married with kids. But my travelling put a stop to that and then I started believing that travel was something that built character, and would help me be the best person I can be. So I continued. I certainly have had an amazing time, but I am still alone and wondering who I am. This was the first time I had actually said this to myself. It was monumental.

Looking back at the London connection that seemed to have broken my heart, I realised now, in hindsight, the reason why it happened. I did see the signs, but I didn't want to acknowledge them. There was another part of his life that he hadn't actually dealt with. I wasn't being honest to myself about what I wanted; that and the fact he was spending lots of time on his issue. We kept going because he kept wanting to see me. I could see that now, in hindsight that whilst he was super nice, maybe he didn't want to share all of his life with me. Maybe he just wasn't really into me, and didn't know what to say. Now that I've met Tom, and seen how truthful someone can be and how open and honest, I don't think the guy from London had the courage to share his true thoughts with me. He wasn't ready. It was hurtful; but I know I am better off without someone who couldn't be honest.

As we continued to see one another and build upon our relationship, Tom became the best friend who supported me no matter what. He didn't let me live in denial and he yanked me out of the holes I was slowly digging myself into. Whilst he was reserved and guarded, at the beginning, once I did get to know him, I discovered a dark, hilarious sense of humour and one of the most loyal friends I know I'll ever meet. Even though there was a beautiful emotional chemistry, and the relationship was delicious and good, I was not able to show up and be my best self.

He knew when it was time to listen, and listening he did amazingly well. He could have been intimidating because he seemed so perfect, but unlike other men I'd met, he wasn't full of himself. He radiated beauty from the inside. He knew how cranky I got, how I looked without make-up, how I love chocolate, and chewed my food. Even though I sure was not perfect, he loved me. He loved my flaws and was there to support me through whatever I faced.

We found we didn't always have to have the same goals, plans, or coping mechanisms. We didn't have the same beliefs, values, priorities, ideas, and interests, but most of them were aligned. He loved animals, and also got a real sense of how much I loved and missed my horses. We were a match made in heaven. And for the rest, we were in our twenties! We knew we needed some room to grow and figure shit out without fear of being condemned.

Finally, I realised I wanted to be treated like a queen by someone special. At long last, I was prepared to open up to someone. I wanted to show up and have someone love me, and treat me with the respect I deserved. We moved in together and bought a puppy to celebrate.

I had to be responsible, and I had decided I was going to invest in myself, and sort out my self-worth, so I booked myself into Relationships Australia to help me find out what the cause was for this pattern. I wanted to shift the pattern. My travels had given me time to work on my self-esteem, and self-forgiveness, and I felt ready. It was hard, it took months of time and action. Yet the end result was I was ready to feel trust and confidence to build upon my relationship.

Falling in love was the easy part. We started as best friends, who appreciated the ocean, fell deeply in love, and had romance sprinkled in between. What happened from that point on was the forming of the best kind of relationship of maturing love. Another thing I found so refreshing was neither of us was needy, or jealous of the other. We did our own thing together, such as diving and were equally comfortable being apart. We found that even if we didn't see or talk to each other on a daily basis, neither of us felt the need to be in constant communication. This man was my rock. I knew he was there for me. When something amazing happened or something shitty happened, he always had my back and he supported me in all that I did.

Even though neither of us were ready for children, marriage was inevitable. We knew that we were a partnership made in heaven. We had differences, yet we knew with effort, we could work as a team to build a life together. Communication was key for us to survive, and whilst we both had that capacity we would do well. Those differences made us unique, and gave us something to discuss and consider. Tom was passionate about his motorbikes, and his dog Eric, and I was passionate about learning. To be honest I was impatient sometimes, and I had to learn to control that, but overall, I think we made a great couple.

Mum would come over and say to me, "When I was your age, I had two small boys to look after. You get things so easy the way you are living. Going off travelling for years, and now studying and working."

I never knew if she meant if I should be having children, or she was just saying there was a difference in the way we live our lives. I did feel the pressure from her, especially when I told her my career was important to me, and I wanted to maintain that for some time. In my mind, she was lucky I had returned, and was settled in a relationship.

THE FARM

A space to grow, to nurture and be.
Where you see the horizon, the moon rise and set, and the stars at night.
Where you hear the frogs, the crickets, and foxes.
See the butterflies, storms, and birds.
Touch the young, the old, and new born

A couple of years into our relationship, we bought a 100 acre farm. We had dreams of making a move to the country, to leave our stressful, underpaid overworked, overcharged life in the city and buy a big property to relax and enjoy. It's something I knew I wanted after being in the UK, and had always thought about it. Many conversations with together made us both realise it wasn't just something we might be able to experience when we retired, it was something we had to make happen. So we did. We bought the farm and decided to build our own shed house on it.

We called it "100 Aker Wood" after Winnie-the-Pooh. The farm was for us both to get away from suburbia and to enjoy the sounds of nature. Yet, as we had to build the shed house it was also many months of sweat and toil. The property was some 150 kms from the city, so it was a place we would go on weekends, and when we had annual leave. It had no electricity or running water, just a dam for stock water, and a place that was flat enough for us to build a shed. We called it the "Block" and it was heaven to both of us.

It was through conversations whilst staying at the "Block" with Tom that I realised I wanted to ride again. One night as we sat around the campfire he convinced me to buy a horse.

"Just to ride around the paddock when we get here," he said. I smiled at him and replied "I'm not sure I will be satisfied with just a ride around the paddock". I knew having that first horse would get me started again with the most wonderful animals alive, and I'd want more than just 'a ride around the paddock'.

Not being one to hold back I started looking straight away and soon found an ex-race horse along with a friend for him. Rabbit and Molly, as they were called, lived on the farm with fresh water and acres to wander in. The 100 acres was filled with wildlife, and Wandoo trees. It had steep hills, echidnas and their puggles, kangaroos and emus. The land had rocky outcrops where you felt like you were on top of the world. You felt you could ride forever across our land and into our neighbours. It was freezing cold in winter and hot and dry in the summer. When the rain came, it caused gullies to form as the water cascaded down the hillside. It had beautiful wildlife and terrain. I loved riding on the land, watching the changes in the flora, smelling the open air and watching the clouds change and race across the sky as the seasons changed. By observing the clouds I could tell when it was going to rain, and if I was riding at the end of our block, I would need to canter home to get unsaddled before the heavens opened up. I would ask Rabbit to traverse the countryside in ways he had never done before. After a long day of working on the shed, Tom and I would saddle them up and ride out in the bush together for hours. It was so blissful. While riding out in the bush I would tune into whatever I would walk past or what came in front of me. Whether that be a bush, a tree, rock, animal, wind or wildflowers. I'd recognise it, and be present with the tree, feel it, see it, and really tune into it as we walked past. This connection with nature allowed me to see lots of wildlife, and lots of minute detail that I knew I was missing in the city. Sadly Rabbit didn't appreciate what I found so lovely, and one day, when we arrived we found he had been caught up in the mud in our dam. He was so badly hurt that he had to be put down.

It didn't take me long to realise I wanted something more from my riding than just enjoying our land. I thought maybe I needed to join a club and get myself another horse. Even though Rabbit hadn't worked out, I decided another ex-race horse would be a good idea. Especially since they were cheap once they had ended their racing career. Another search and I soon found a chestnut gelding called George, who had come off-the-track. The time away from competing with my horses had done me good. Whilst I still had a "good seat" with the ability to sit tall and straight in the saddle and ride, there was a change in the way I looked at horses. As an adult, I believed there was a better way to "be" with the horses than what I knew from when I was a teen. I knew some of the practices that I did in the past were perhaps not the best for the welfare of horses, and I wanted to change.

As my husband is not really a "horsey man" I connected with the people from the local riding clubs. Here I watched and listened. I sought out riders I admired, in the level I knew I could achieve, and started to ask them for advice. I wanted a better understanding of the horse and how we ride them, and I made friends with coaches and professional riders. I wanted to know all there was, and sought a coach who was committed to helping me become the rider I dreamt of being.

George and I began our exploration of natural horsemanship techniques, specifically in the area of groundwork. We practised working together in-hand, at liberty, and on a lunge line. During our liberty work, I was pleased to see George display some beautiful gaits and a strong sense of his body positioning, for the most part. These positive results kept me motivated to continue our training. However, when it came to riding, it was a different story altogether. Despite his impeccable manners on the ground, things changed once I mounted him and it was a totally different experience.

I joined a dressage club and believed the instruction would benefit my riding and support my horse with the development of his balance and flexibility. I was learning rapidly that race horses are ridden in a straight line, and always in the same direction, and this impacted on how I needed to ride him. From going in the one direction all the time, he favoured one side, and was actually not very flexible at all.

I also had to learn about the impact of training on a race horse and how that related to me riding him. For example, I soon learnt that if you shortened the reins, to a racehorse, that meant that it was time to gallop. George was no different. He would walk quietly on a long rein, but the minute I picked them up to do some work, he'd panic or want to gallop off. There seemed to be a fine line between having just enough control, and giving him the impression I wanted to win a race. It was a conundrum that had me questioning my ability to be with horses.

Over time, George and I learnt how we each operated and I started to take him to events. At first, they were simple adult riding competitions where just getting out was a huge feat. I got myself a new saddle to fit him properly and we really started to make progress. He was soon doing dressage and it became clear that he loved jumping. I was keen to get out and compete with him, and entered a few competitions to see how he went. Each time I took him out, it was hard work. When he was removed from his usual surroundings he became anxious, and was a horse that needed constant minding. When standing at the float, and when being ridden he was prone to spooking, or bucking or stopping suddenly and trying to get me off. Regardless I kept going, I wanted to help. There were days when he was really very sweet and willing and aimed to please. For me it was a challenge to 'fix'.

I had to treat him like he was a youngster, as everything he saw was new to him. There were simple things, like being tied up or walking to a mounting block that would make him react wildly. He had not known these before so they were all foreign to him. In fact, I found out that in racing stables the riders are mounted whilst the horse is walking - so the horses never know how to stand whilst being mounted. I rode him with the aim of improving our relationship, yet I was also continually challenged by him. Whilst I practised regularly, and was committed to improving, not much changed. I genuinely hoped that, given time, I would reap the rewards of my hard work and achieve my own level of success with this horse.

George was not an easy horse to ride because he had come from a racing stable, and whilst he could gallop fast in a straight line, he didn't much like the dressage or show jumping rings. I would try a number of ways to ride him, in the hope that something would gel with him, but just like with my English teacher in my last year of school, it didn't matter what I did, he would take umbrage with it. I would take him out to the bush to ride, and he would hate the noises and the kangaroos that bounced across the path; he would often buck when I first mounted him, or took off at a gallop for no apparent reason. I had been dumped in the bush, broken my hand from one of the many falls, walked home alone, and realised I needed to be safer. No longer was I that invincible person who could do anything!

One rainy day at the riding club, one of the male riders came up to me and suggested that George should go barefoot. He had been walking past the float at the time, and as he headed towards his float he looked George up and down, and then simply came out with it. I was offended at first and said under my breath "who does he think he is criticising my horse's feet". Admittedly, he did need to have them done, and by the length on his toe, he was two weeks overdue for a trim and being reshod. I buried my face into the float and ignored the comment. Fiddling with my saddle, I heard feet nearby.

"His feet, whilst long, appear from here that they could benefit from being barefoot" said the man, who I soon learned was Michael, husband to Julie. Julie was riding in the lesson happening in the arena and Michael had just finished his.

He continued and explained how the horse's hooves are restricted whilst they are in shoes, and going barefoot is not about the foot alone; it was about improving the horse's overall well being. He talked about blood-flow and that studies showed the horse's foot gets at least twice as much circulation when they are barefoot on yielding terrain, as compared to when they are wearing a metal shoe.

He picked up one of George's hooves to explain more about the way it moved. "See this bit here, the back part of the foot? It is designed to flex, twist and distort with uneven terrain and when doing turns," he said. "So when they are barefoot it helps reduce stress and prevent injury to joints, ligaments and tendons." He put the hoof down and continued, "and the restrictive nature of metal shoes stops that from happening".

I was fascinated.

"Does he stumble much? I saw he did a couple of times out in the arena today" asked Michael.

"Yes, he does, come to think of it. I had thought he was a klutz, or maybe something to do with being a thoroughbred" I replied.

"Maybe" Michael mused "I think it could be his feet are sore though, or restricted in the shoes"

"Really! Goodness I'd never thought of that" I said. I had just gone along with the theory that horses needed metal shoes on their feet. I was told that as a child, and it happened in the UK, and I never questioned it. Barefoot was not something I had even come across in my riding, but I reflected that wild horses are barefoot, so they can cope. Michael broke into my thoughts.

"You'll only know if you give it a go," he said

I smiled and started considering the whole concept.

When I got home from the riding club later that day, I jumped onto the computer and started to research it myself. Julie emailed me a heap of articles and after a few days I decided I would try to move him to barefoot, and perhaps that would help him and maybe stop the bucking. My interest in having barefooted horses grew and I read many articles, spoke to others and found out about the many benefits of going barefoot. Through my experience, I discovered that the benefits of a particular technique would vary depending on the horse. However, I learned that the benefits included improved circulation to the feet, better traction, enhanced movement, and stronger, healthier hoof growth. All of this convinced me to do it. The first thing was to take his shoes off, so I called the farrier and asked him to come over as soon as he could. He came the next day, and I paid him for his time.

It was a new concept for me and I soon found out I had jumped in blindly. Nevertheless, I could see the benefits, and wanted to help my horse. As soon as the shoes came off though, he became sore. Realising that adjusting from shod to barefoot wasn't as simple as removing his shoes and hoping for the best, I needed to think through a strategy.

I spoke to Julie about it, and she agreed that I should buy him some rubber horse boots to help him. I bought the most expensive rubber boots specially made for horse's hooves, and put them on to support him when we went out in the bush, or on any hard ground. The plan to avoid his foot soreness, meant a transition from metal shoes, to the rubber boots and finally he would be able to walk just on his hooves. It was a slow process, because as a horse that had been shod all his life, he needed some time to acclimatise to this new way of being. Just like if we were to go from wearing slippers all day to walking barefoot across the gravel drive or a road, our feet would be ripped to shreds, and we would have blisters for months. A horse's hoof is naturally harder than our tender skinned feet, but I thought that explanation made sense when I spoke to others about it. His hooves were tender in the early stages, and it took many months for them to get to the point where the farrier could begin to reshape them, rather than just trimming them. In all, the full transition process from shod to barefoot took nearly a year.

Whilst overall, I believed he reacted very well to the barefoot approach, I would occasionally require the farrier to come and put on some front shoes because his feet were reacting to the weather changes, or hard surface on the ground. I knew this was all part of the process. I considered it as part of a holistic approach for my horse, one that included management, feeding and exercise in addition to the barefoot trim. The approach in itself was something that got me really considering the way I had been taught to be with horses. The way people said, "this is what you MUST do" and I had just unquestioningly followed that advice. So now I was seeing that the relationship I had with them was more important than the attitude that was so often instilled in me to, "make them just do it." I knew I was on the journey to a better way.

When riding, George reacted well to the barefoot trimming and he appeared to be moving more naturally. I also noticed he developed better muscle tone quickly, which I put down to his new way of moving. Our instructor at the riding club had commented saying how much better he seemed. "Whatever you are doing, keep doing it." I was told in one lesson. His gaits improved, and he stumbled less frequently, and the bucking reduced after the barefoot trim.

The path was slow, yet it was enjoyable, and George was a keen jumper. He quickly moved from the smaller jumps to competing at a height where the moment of being airborne was a thrilling experience. As I had only recently come back into the sport of riding horses, having had a few years away from them, this was exhilarating for me. In my teenage years, I had competed in show jumping to a very successful level every weekend, which meant I was mentally and physically fit. When I was in the United Kingdom I rode a friend's horse in a couple of competitions, but I spent much of my time travelling. So having put riding on hold to have fun and explore, I actually thought I would never ride those amazing cross country jumps again. Feeling George want to jump gave me the impetus to work hard on both of us.

On a weekend in June, I was competing George at an event in the Swan Valley. He had been barefoot for over a year and was doing well with it. We had done our dressage earlier that morning and were warming up in a crowded ring for the show jumping phase of the 95cm class. It was wet on the ground, with rain filling my eyes, and George was full of himself. He was trotting sideways, and racing up to the fences, which could be dangerous in the best of times, let alone when it was a wet slippery arena. With all the horses in the ring I needed to keep our warm-up low key. As I readied myself to jump over the last practice fence, I took a quick glance around the arena to ensure that no other riders were coming towards me. Sometimes, other riders would unknowingly ride their horses in your direction, and it was important to remain vigilant. After ensuring that the way was clear, I approached the jump while keeping a firm hold on George's reins. The way was clear so I approached the jump and held George together, clearing it easily.

As I landed after the jump, my eyes locked onto a magnificent black and white horse. George often had a tendency to do something to try to get me off after a fence, so I quickly went back to focusing on him. When I had George under control, I snuck another look at that beautiful black and white horse. He was stunning, and I knew right then that this horse was special and I felt a growing desire to own him. I chided myself for the ridiculousness of my thought, but nonetheless wanted to check him out some more. I forced myself to concentrate on George and what we were doing. My riding skills to this point had improved, but I still needed to concentrate with this horse. We finished the day successfully, I stayed on, he stayed in the arena, and we had a score at the end, rather than a DNF. I was pleased with our efforts and put the weekend down to be being a success.

At the end of the day, when the scores were tallied up and the winners announced, I made a point of finding out the name of the magnificent horse and saw it was Bundy Bear. Bundy and his rider were just a couple of points ahead of our result, but neither of us were in the placings. Even though I tried not to think of him there was definitely a pull to find out more.

RELATIONSHIPS

We are put here on earth to be in relationship.
Relationship with self, with other, and with animal and plants.
It is essential for our life.

As my relationship evolved into marriage, it had its fair share of ups and downs, and work took up a significant portion of my life. To maintain my sanity, I turned to horse riding as a way to relax. Unfortunately, George was a nervous horse, so riding him didn't provide the stress-relieving escape I was looking for. Despite this, I persisted in my efforts to strengthen my relationship with George and improve our outcomes.

I had seen a demonstration at Riding Club about natural horsemanship, which essentially was a better way of working with your horse. So I decided to book into a clinic the following weekend. The two days were long and slow, yet I did come away with some new tips and ways of looking at my horse. There were many hours where we would be shown how to do something and then be asked to do it ourselves with our horses, and then we would all stand in the hot sun and watch whilst others tried to get a handle of it. Then after an hour or so of doing that we would take the horses back to the float and we would sit and watch another class.

It was the waiting around for your next session that took the longest. The first day I had taken a note book with me, so I would sit and watch the others, and write down what I observed. I'd recall what we'd been told in the lesson, and then try to recap it. I needed to do this so that I could remember what to practice when I got home.

One of these practises we had been shown was to match my steps with my horse, which was designed to build a better connection between the rider and the horse. I had practiced this on Saturday and then again on Sunday in the company of others, and with an instructor who would remind me of things I'd forgotten. We hadn't made the connection yet, however I had seen it in other riders with their horses. It was a beautiful sight.

So I wanted to practice it straight away whilst the memory was strong. That night as I went to bed I took my note book with me and read through my notes. "I have to get this right," I said to myself before closing the book and turning off the light. The next morning, I woke early to take George out for a walk before I left for work. The purpose of the walk was to try to practice our steps, and match his pace. The result I wanted was a more connected horse. That was the theory. Now, he is a fast walker and when I did this, all I could hear was the monkey in my head getting frustrated at how fast he was walking - oh now I'm falling behind, is that a problem, is this dangerous, am I going to get hurt, what I am having for lunch, what do I have to do at work this week, how fast he walks, how excruciating this was and how excruciating it is just like when I sit down to do meditation practises… blah blah blah. The thoughts kept coming and George and I were no more connected than when we headed out.

Disappointed, I put him away and got ready for work. As I drove down the hill, I contemplated what had happened. I could clearly see that I wanted a result fast, but that morning's exercise highlighted to me just how impatient I was. I really wanted to get this practise right as I'd heard that 'matching steps' is so powerful. I wanted that energetic synchronicity that I'd seen others have with their horse. There must be some magic way of getting this right. All these thoughts had got me agitated, and along with the heavy traffic and idiot drivers on the road, by the time I reached the office I was angry. I stormed in and sat down at my chair grumpy with myself for not being able to work it out. Not being able to get this horse into submission. Whether it was coincidence or good planning, bizarrely people stayed away from me all day.

In this journey of change I so wanted to be a compassionate rider, it was almost becoming an obsession. Yet, even though I had read the theory, been to the clinics, and really believed I had been trying hard to connect, George and I didn't really get along. I didn't actually know what happened in racing stables, yet I had heard many sad stories about other horses, and in my naive way I lumped those stories onto George. I had learnt so much about ways of working with him so that he would stop and listen to me, rather than grab hold of the bit and run away. I had worked hard on getting his stiff and resistant body to be more flexible, and supple. We'd worked hard on standing still when being mounted - all areas that are common with ex-race horses. Yet George seemed troubled, and even though I wanted to help him, I seemed to be running out of ideas. We weren't connecting and I was giving up. During this process my own emotional wellbeing and confidence was slowly going downhill. Plus, the time, energy and financial costs I had already invested in George had been immense.

Then one day, just after I had returned from the hospital where my father was suffering a long illness, I realised it was silly to continue with a horse who wouldn't connect to me. It was like we were both going along on parallel paths, and ones that would never cross. I was in my car, having driven for three hours and as I turned off the main highway into the road that connected to our village, I started to cry as I considered the realisation. Not just small tears, but huge fat hot and heavy tears. I was a soaking mess of tears. My face filled up, and I could hardly see as I drove down the road, so I pulled over to the side to find a tissue, and get myself together so I could drive home safely.

As I drove into the yard and parked my car, I started sobbing again. My husband came out to meet me, and he could see straight away that I was distraught. At first he thought it was because of my Dad. Thinking the worst, he was concerned I had driven all that way in such a state. Finally, when I was out of the car and able to speak, I told him it was about George, and maybe because of the stress from Dad's illness.

We talked it over for some time, and Tom said "maybe it was his personality, and we just clashed."

"Yeah, could be," I replied "not all people get along, and so maybe it was the same with horses. Who knows what it is, I'm just not feeling his love anymore"

"It's OK to feel that Amanda," said Tom soothing my nerves "I know you are trying to do the right thing with him. Maybe someone else will have a better go"

"You're right, it's just so hard to think he is going to someone else and will have to get used to them and all." I said.

"He'll be okay. He's a horse. There are some awesome people out there." Tom said in a tone that had me guessing if he was actually joking or not.

"Put him on the market and see what happens. That will tell you if it is the right thing to do," Tom said.

Even though the thought of finding a new horse quietly excited me, I said, "and then comes the long process of locating a new horse, and seeing if we connect"

As I walked away I felt I had known this for a long time but was too scared that Tom would stop me from selling him. I had made up stories that Tom would say I needed to keep my horse for life, as so often was the need in the horse community. The relief of knowing that my husband supported me in the sale was amazing. I promptly went about putting George on the market to be sold, and started looking for a new partner.

LOOKING FOR A NEW HORSE

The endorphin rush of buying something new.
The excitement of the changes it can make to you and your life.

On a horse buy and sell website, I searched for horses around my price range. When I had been searching for a horse before I found George, I knew about an app on the internet that was all about selling horses, ponies and related equipment. I logged in and used the search function to narrow my search down to my budget, and a rough size of horse. This way I wasn't looking at amazing horses that were totally beyond my budget! It was times like these that I wondered if I was experienced enough to know what horse to buy. I chastised myself as I knew I had managed to work my way to being in a leadership role in my job, I had travelled the world by myself and I had found myself an amazing man. And here I was worrying over buying a horse.

Even so, the money I earned was still relatively small, and I didn't feel I could spend too much on a new horse. So I considered different options about whether I could find a horse that was not too expensive, and one I could bring on over a period of time, rather than having a horse ready to go and compete straight away.

I spent many evenings looking, messaging people and getting no response. Or getting told something and then when I went out to view the horse it had a sway back, or was lame, was skittish to the point of being dangerous, or was so drugged up it didn't move. After two months of searching, and going out to ride horses that I didn't connect with, I became quite frustrated.

In that time, I met many wannabe owners for George and eventually settled on selling him for a reasonable price, to a lovely lady. I had actually got him to a good state and we had competed successfully at 95cm; she rode him a couple of times and felt comfortable with him. She had him vet checked and he passed. As he left the gate with his new owners, there were mixed emotions and I wondered if I was doing the right thing. Maybe I should have held onto him and put some more effort in, maybe we could have made it together. And strongest of all, the feeling of yearning for the unreachable, and wondering if I would ever find the right horse.

That evening I searched the internet again, but this time I searched for all horses that were on the market, rather than just the ones in my price range. And there, right in front of me, was Bundy Bear, that beautiful horse I had met some months before in the warm up arena. He was listed for a huge amount of money, well out of my budget. Even with the money I had got from the sale of George, this was an extraordinary price for a horse, I thought, and it was way beyond my price range. I knew I could never ask my husband to agree to pay that for any horse, no matter how much I loved him. Owning the horses was my joy, and as we both worked, I felt responsible for paying for the purchase.

The weeks ticked by and I kept searching for a new partner, but, frustratingly, nothing showed its face. Then one day, I noticed that Bundy Bear's selling price had been reduced quite substantially. He was still over my price range, but he was more accessible now. I knew deep down that I needed to share a path with that beautiful yet clearly troubled soul, even though I didn't have any idea where I'd find the money.

Life, working in that mysterious way it does sometimes, had me brought to the head of Human Resources just two weeks later, and they told me they'd made a mistake on my commission from a job that I had worked on, and I therefore was owed a substantial amount of money.

"Wahoo!" I wanted to yell, as I walked out of the office, with a ear to ear grin that said everything I couldn't shout. Instead of yelling, I walked out the back door of the office and threw my hands in the air, clicking my heels together, then ran out onto the grassed area behind the building. Luckily, no one from the office could see this area from their windows, nor was it filled with smokers, as it could sometimes be. My smile hadn't left my face, and I sat down on a bench that smokers used, stunned from what I'd just heard. I considered my options; should I call Tom and tell him now, or wait till I see it in my bank? I picked up my phone and dialled his number.

"Hiya," I said jumping from foot to foot like I was on hot coals, "guess what?"

"God knows." he replied "You've been promoted?"

"Almost. Remember that project I worked on last year and I was sure they had short changed me on my commission?" I said as I stood up and started to walk around with the phone glued to my ear.

"Yes, the one with that big recruitment firm?" he asked.

"That's the one. Well, I was called into HR today and told me they had realised they had made a mistake and I was owed money..." I paused to let that sink in.

"How much?"

"Over ten grand!" I whispered so that no one could hear.

"Far out, that is fantastic!" came his reply.

I did a little dance and laughed into the phone receiver "See you tonight. Love you." and I rung off.

With this little windfall, I could now increase the amount of money I could spend on my new horse. Tom didn't even question it.

He said to me that evening as he was preparing dinner, "You've earned it darling, it's yours."

So now Bundy Bear was in my price range, and very soon, he came to live with Tom and me.

Almost immediately, life changed for Bundy Bear and all who met him. He had embarked on a journey that would take him from that vulnerable dark place to a place where he could be the courageous being he was deep inside. From that first moment of burying my face into his gentle muzzle, I knew I'd done the right thing. The smell of freshly baked biscuits wafted through my nostrils. It went down to my soul. That smell you get when you bury your face into a horse's muzzle was something so right, so wonderful.

He wasn't easy, he was big and he had huge issues. He would walk through me, and disrespected what I asked. His eyes were shut down, and he seemed to act on auto pilot. When I asked him to lunge he galloped around in circles, totally scared of the whole situation he was in. I could see from the minute I brought him to my place that it was going to be a huge undertaking. I had no idea just how long that would be.

As I learned to work with him, I ultimately learned about myself.

GEORGE

In embracing true listening, we open ourselves to a wealth of wisdom in our surroundings. Conversely, when we close ourselves off and act impulsively, we inadvertently pave a longer and more challenging path for ourselves.

A few months after I bought Bundy Bear, I was in Bunbury, a country town south of Perth, supporting my mother after Dad's passing. It had just been a day since he passed. I was in the kitchen, clearing up the lunch dishes. Everything was a blur, and it had been that way for the past three days. We had been going into the hospital daily, and finally after a long battle with cancer and emphysema, Dad had passed on. As I wiped the dishes, my mobile rang and I looked across to the kitchen table where it sat. The screen read "George owner." It was Sandra, the lady who had bought George, so I answered it. I'm not sure why, I think I wanted something normal to talk about, something that lit me up, and horses generally did that.

Sandra started explaining that George had not been well and they had spent a lot of money at the vets. I was sad to hear this, and even sadder as I was currently in a state of grieving. "God", I thought, "why did I take this call? She is just going to bag him out to me." The person on the other end of the phone explained that George was suffering the effects of navicular disease, a disease that ate away at the horse's foot. It was extremely painful, and they had decided not to rehabilitate the horse. They said they had no option but to put George to sleep. I wanted to scream! I couldn't because I was still standing in the kitchen and the house was filled with family and well-wishers and screaming would upset everyone. So I walked outside to the patio and sat on one of the chairs. The air was cool but I felt hot. I asked them what they had done to his feet once they had purchased him. She said they had him shod on all four feet immediately, as she was not able to manage him being barefoot. I was furious, and knew that the reason he was suffering was that she had shod him again. I said nothing. I couldn't. I was so drained.

In desperation to keep the horse alive, I called my friend Julie and spoke to her at length. After I got off the phone, Julie and Michael considered the situation. We all believed George could be returned to health by being barefoot again, along with other treatment. Julie called me back within an hour and asked for Sandra's phone number so that she could call her and explain the situation. Sadly George's owners decided it wasn't worth it, and they put him to sleep the next day. In my grief ridden state, I was not in any position to argue and try to change their decision.

When Dad's funeral was over and Mum's house was tidied up, we removed all of Dad's belongings (random I know – yet it was Mum's choice), then I had time to think about George. It was sad that a horse's life was lost, although we had thought we could help him. I called Julie and spoke to her again, and she helped me realise just how much pain George must have been in before we took his shoes off. With horses it is hard to understand the whole truth of what is happening, and sadly I understood this too late. I could see that the barefoot and corrective trimming he received whilst with me had helped him. At the time, I had no idea about navicular disease; however, now I could see that this natural method of foot care, rather than putting shoes on him, was effective for his pain relief.

Julie shared some articles with me, and I read how horses with this disease suffered from poor development of the internal structures in the back of the foot. This is exactly what Michael had told me back at the riding club. The constant natural pressure and release from being barefoot impacted the bottom of the hoof, and the flexion of the hoof capsule eased these structural issues. I knew I had helped a poor soul, and I vowed I would continue to have my horses barefoot whenever I could.

When Bundy Bear first arrived he had all four feet shod, and it didn't take me long to find a farrier who could remove his shoes, so that I could see how he went. He had amazing feet, and it didn't take him long to adjust to being barefoot. The boots I had used for George were too small for Bundy's huge feet, so I bought him some bigger boots to help him during the process. Julie helped me learn the art of trimming his feet myself, and through this I could understand more about the horse and the effects of their feet on the whole body. Being young and fit I was more than happy to learn new skills to support my horse and his well-being.

CONTINUOUS LEARNING

To stop learning is to stop living. You might as well be dead.

Soon after Bundy Bear came to my place, I knew that the best thing I could do for my horse was to really work on my riding and horsemanship skills. This horse needed my support much more than any other horse I'd known. He was scarred from his previous life and needed someone to help him. George had given me some excellent skills to commence the journey, but I knew there was so much more to learn. I joined another local Riding Club, and took as many lessons as I could afford. At night I would watch DVDs, read books, and search out experts and their opinions in articles and on YouTube. I was curious and I was driven to learn. My experience with George told me there was so much more I needed to learn.

Just like the new holistic approach I was taking with my horse, I took the same approach with myself. I used to rely on my youth as a way to keep fit, but now I decided my body needed a different approach. Riding isn't just a sport of fitness, like running or a sport of strength like lifting, it's about balance and coordination, as well as fitness and strength. I took yoga and Zumba classes to keep myself fit and flexible, and to ensure I was ready for whatever came along.

Initially, my intention was to compete with Bundy Bear one day, but I soon learned that he wasn't going to be a horse that I could just get on and ride at a competition immediately. He had baggage, and for him to be able to compete, he needed to feel confident in himself and in our partnership together. He needed a good foundation, something solid to fall back on when things got tough, and someone that would always be there to support him.

As I looked at his broad forehead and bright, intelligent eyes, I got the sense that there was some strong connection to the earth. Yet, this horse outwardly showed fear. He physically shared with me how he felt, through his nervousness, his wild looking eyes, and his need to gallop off constantly. I wanted to reach that deeper side of him, to allow him to relax, and enjoy. That meant I needed to take time to get to know him, and to allow him to trust me. So rather than setting a goal that reflected time, I decided I would take the training when he told me he was ready. I still held tight to my goals to compete, but it was "one day" now, rather than setting a specific timeline. I had to wait until Bundy Bear was ready.

I wanted to understand Bundy Bear more, and to do that I needed a reference - something I had learnt before, so I could apply that to how I imagined a horse worked. I didn't want to try to teach him English, I wanted to understand what he wanted, and his language. I practised the 'matching steps' idea with Bundy Bear, the one I couldn't get to work with George. It took us a couple of goes, but I could almost instantly feel a change with him. The change was subtle, yet it was so powerful, with a kind of energetic synchrony. It was a way of saying to him that I had his back, and we would work on this together. I could feel this was the beginning of a better relationship, of building trust and something stronger than ever. I knew Bundy had come from a station, which told me he had been taught the way of being a wild animal, and I had to respect this. Even though he lived in my yard, he was himself, and had his individual needs and wants.

Horses are known for having a brilliant memory, and especially a recognition memory. They don't reflect on the past as we can, or project into the future, yet they can recognise stimuli. For instance, when they are hit with a whip they remember it.

The experience had a fascinating impact on me. It felt as if an old memory was resurfacing, and we all seemed to merge into one entity, transcending the boundaries of being human or horse. It made me question the conventional norms of society and how they hindered my personal fulfilment. I believed that this experience would contribute to a more enriching life. Later that evening, while discussing it with Tom, I asked him about the changes I was undergoing.

"I know this could be hard for you to say, but I really want to know if you have noticed a change in me?" I started

"What do you mean, I love you just the way you are," Tom replied.

"I know darling, I just want to know if you have seen any difference in the way I react," I said trying again.

"Oh yes, don't take this the wrong way, but you can be so impatient sometimes. When you have an idea, you want it right now! I've noticed that it is lessening, you are more going with the flow."

I wanted to ask so many questions to clarify what he was actually saying but asked instead, "so is that a good thing?"

"It sure is, and I think that is what Bundy is picking up on," he said

Forever the intuitive man, Tom had nailed it

"I think that is a good thing what you've just said. And somewhat a reminder. Thanks so much for being honest with me. It helps me understand." I replied.

Just like I had done with George, I created a new vision board that showed a black and white horse being ridden over cross country jumps and in dressage. Before I started, I looked back at the one that showed a chestnut horse jumping a fence that looked like it could have been at one of the big Western Australian three day events. It looked like the jump was 95cm, and the horse and rider were flying over it, having a wonderful time. That, I thought to myself, is exactly what we did. We achieved that, plus more.

The vision boards I've created are a visual display of what I want to bring to life. I have found over the years, and through the research I've done, that what we focus on expands. I can see the images daily, and the vision board brings my goals and aspirations to life. So it was important for me to put my goals on my board.

FEAR

Our emotions are chemical reactions.
What our body does with that reaction is what we know as an emotional response.
Awareness gives as choice.

Whilst I had a feeling of synchronicity, I still wasn't able to help Bundy with his fear response. During my studies, I had learned that fear is a normal human emotion that comes when our brain refers back to, or re-lives, past experiences. The fear is our thoughts imagining what will happen in the future, based on what happened in the past and our reactions and behaviours that relate to that experience. It appeared at the outset that Bundy had many experiences, and ones I was yet to find out about.

In the workplace as a leader I felt it was important to really understand people so they would perform at their best. Being a young leader meant I didn't know much about leadership, but I was hell bent on finding out as much as I could to help my team, and how that would help me too, as the leader. I asked my boss for some help, but he just told me to 'suck it up'. No help there.

Okay, I thought, there must be another way. So I tried to find out about my team's life outside of work so that I could be more understanding and compassionate when they asked for time off. I searched the internet for ideas, but there was limited information that I could find to help me. What was there I devoured and tried with my team. I was in this learning mode, and tried various concepts that seemed to work. For me, life was a continuous study and learning experience.

My studies continued every Thursday evening where I would attend a lecture at a campus about forty minutes' drive away from home. It was on the way from work, so it just meant I didn't see the horses that evening. I grabbed a bite at a takeaway place, and headed straight to college. We had received an email earlier in the day that told us that this evening's lecture was about human emotions.

"Awesome," I said to one of my fellow students as we walked into the room. "This is exactly what I need to hear tonight." I settled in at a desk for some serious learning.

"Fear is not all bad, it can also be fun, or exciting," Mr Chakra, our lecturer said to us.

"Fear is something that everyone has. It is an emotion that tries to keep you safe. Sometimes that fear is based on a traumatic experience, and sometimes it is based on a negative experience. The experience could be something that actually happened, like riding a bike and falling off and breaking your leg. Or it could be something someone said, like a story or movie that has frightened you, and then it percolated in your mind and got bigger over time. These experiences, whilst small or minor at the time, could become larger and larger as time goes on, and with validation, it could become huge in the mind of the person.

Fear is essential for our survival. People generally consider fear as an unpleasant emotion, and try to avoid it. Some people, however, actually go out of their way to trigger it. Think about scary fairground rides, and rock climbing."

He looked at the class and then spoke to the room, *"Has anyone ever jumped out of an aeroplane?"*

James's hand shot up and he yelled, "I love watching horror movies!"

"*Yes,*" said Mr Chakra "that is common; we sometimes love to experience the rush of terror while watching a horror movie, even though we know that the villain or monster is an actor in makeup and that the blood is not real. We get drawn in by the sounds and images which in turn create emotions."

The room buzzed with conversation about the ways people seek fear. We were prompted to share our experiences with our fellow students. Sitting beside me was Mario, who opened up about his love for skydiving and how fear affects him. He recounted his first time, getting suited up and receiving the safety brief. He said, "I didn't really want to jump, and during the safety brief, all I heard were reasons why I shouldn't go through with it. But I pushed forward, got into the plane with the others, all of us avoiding eye contact to hide our shared fear. When the plane door opened, I realised I was up next. As I looked down, facing the possibility of death, I hesitated after one and two, but then I was pushed into the air. And there, floating in the sky, I experienced the most blissful feeling of my life. There was no fear, just being completely present in that moment."

A smile formed on his face, and he added, almost dreamily, "The best things in life are on the other side of fear. That's why I keep going back."

I shared with him something that was similar. When I was learning to scuba dive, and I was terrified of being below the water, the fear was real for me, and it took many minutes of coaching from my instructor before I was comfortable putting my head underneath water. Even though I am now a scuba diver with many hours in my log book, I still get that fear. But the blissful floating in the water and seeing fish and creatures I only ever see on TV, far outweighed the stories I heard in my head.

As Mr. Chakra resumed the lecture on the origins of fear, my mind raced with thoughts and connections. I felt compelled to jot down my ideas, reflecting on instances where I had observed fear in my staff and even in my horse. The concept fascinated me. While riding my horse, I had never experienced any harm. Yet, many people regarded riding cross country jumps as scary and considered me brave for attempting it. Every time I took Tom along to walk the cross country course with me, he would comment on the size of the jumps and express concern for my safety. Initially, I brushed it off with laughter, but those fleeting thoughts lingered in my mind. Gradually, they grew more substantial, and I found myself questioning whether eventing was the right pursuit for me.

Mr Chakra went on, "It is thought that fear has been part of our success as a species. Fear has enabled our ancestors to run and hide from bigger animals or dangerous situations, keeping them safe. The ones that didn't feel the fear were more likely removed from the gene pool before they could procreate.

Fear arises in our body. When someone feels threatened, their body prepares them for attack. It activates a small organ in the middle of your brain called the amygdala, which in turn increases body functions such as breathing, pumping extra blood to the heart, and preparing to run away. It is sometimes called the flight, fight or freeze reaction. We either flee the scene, fight back or become immobile. Sometimes fear can overtake our emotions and our thoughts and behaviours, which is then displayed as anxiety, stress and in some cases being stuck in a negative pattern.

In humans, the same process happens, along with a reduction of blood to areas such as the prefrontal cortex, the "thinking" brain. All the blood is preparing the body to flee, and going to areas to support that response. This means when fear happens to a human, they have limited capacity to process the information given to them, making it difficult to make good decisions or think clearly. Sometimes our body makes a response we are not conscious of, and this is why immediate reactions such as screaming, yelling or hiding cannot be rationalised." I stopped writing for a moment and tuned back in to hear Mr Chakra continuing.

"When watching scary movies the hippocampus and prefrontal cortex or thinking brain can dial the natural response back and still have heightened senses, and the rush, but not in an overly emotional way. In the animal kingdom many small animals freeze before they decide what to do. When they are well-camouflaged, staying still saves their life. Other animals such as wild horses and zebras are prey animals and their response is to take flight. They gallop away from the predator."

"Oh my god," I thought "that makes so much sense!"

This is exactly what I had seen in Bundy Bear, and now it was making sense to me. When Bundy Bear was in his herd, the herd would rely on fear to know if a tree was going to fall on them, or a snake was about to bite, or a wild boar wanted to eat them. Their response would be to gallop away. If he didn't like the look of something, he would freeze, and stare at it, and maybe snort, until he was certain it wouldn't attack him. His response to fear, just like in humans, has to do with the context of the situation. This, and the vigilance of the other herd members kept him safe.

I sat at the desk contemplating what he had said and thought about riding a cross country course, and how my fear arises in me as I warm my horse up. I considered how fear pumps me up when I enter a competition, or when I arrive at the grounds with my horse still in the float. Those butterflies in my stomach as I prepare the float with all of the gear, ready to leave early the next morning for the competition - that is all fear in various forms helping me to get through the next event about to happen. I feel in my horse his heightened fear as he starts to jog, and throw his head around.

"Fear is a complex human emotion that can be both positive and healthy in certain contexts, and negative in others," he went on. "It is powerful and can have strong effects on your body and your mind. When it appears in non-threatening events such as taking my exams it appears real."

Or, in my case, when I was preparing the float for a competition, I thought.

"But that is just your mind making it seem real. Sometimes this 'reality' stops us from moving forward, or from thinking properly, he went on. Fearing failure can be good and bad. When you recognise it, you can use it so that you don't fail. However, it can also be so immobilising that it stops you, and your thinking in your tracks, which stops you from moving forward, and inevitably makes you fail! Just like when you are so afraid of failing at something that you decided not to try at all. Many of us have probably experienced this at one time or another. When we allow fear to stop our forward progress in life, we're likely to miss some great opportunities along the way."

"Oh, now I get it," I said out loud, when I meant to say it to myself. Oops. Did I really say that? I looked around the room to see if anyone heard me. Luckily it appeared no one did or they chose to ignore it.

"So the trick is to recognise fear before it creates anxiety and stops you in your tracks," Mr Chakra continued. I was tuning back in now.

To me, fear heightened my senses so that I could prepare better for my events. It reminded me of everything that needed to be loaded up, and the logistics of getting to the event. When all of this was planned out in my mind, then I would feel safe and ready.

While working with Bundy, I couldn't help but notice his strong fear reactions to various activities we engaged in together. Unlike a visible scar or an expressive tattoo on someone's arm, his fear wasn't apparent on the surface. Perhaps because it went unnoticed, people didn't recognise the need to address or tend to it. But I did. I knew there was something behind his fear, and I pondered whether it stemmed from his past experiences with humans or from his time on the station, or perhaps a combination of both. It could be the frustration of no longer being able to do what he once could, like galloping freely with his herd. He still felt the fear, his instinct to protect himself kicking in, but he was now unable to escape it. When he first arrived at our stable, I noticed his initial response was to attempt galloping away. However, over time, I witnessed his fear manifest as freezing in place and his entire body becoming rigid. He refused to move forward, standing there immobile with his head held high and ears pricked. It seemed as though he was deeply troubled and uncertain how to react. It was evident that Bundy Bear had experienced numerous painful and sorrowful moments, leading him to shut down as a means of self-preservation. He learned that by not speaking out, not retaliating, or responding negatively, he could create a sense of safety. It became a survival mechanism for him. I recalled what I'd learnt about how human brains try to keep us safe in the same way.

This fear was important because when it arises in your body it gives you the survival instincts you need to keep yourself safe from danger. It tells you something about a threat and then you have a choice to react. Without fear, you wouldn't live very long because you wouldn't be aware of or care about the threats around you. In the horse world, this meant that they could gallop to safety if something threatened them.

I recall times when I heard that little voice in my head that said, "Don't do that I...it's not safe" or "maybe not today, maybe you don't need to say that..." or something similar. Now I knew that these voices were there to keep me safe. Yet I recognised it as fear, something that everyone gets, including horses, and other animals.

"Are horses the same?" I thought. "Do they also hear voices in their heads?" I wondered if that is what was happening with Bundy Bear, or Mr Bear as I sometimes called him.

One winter's day very early in our relationship, I brought Bundy into the yard so that I could work with him on some simple skills, like responding to the whip that is used as an extension of my hand and not as a tool to beat him with, moving sideways, backwards and forward when asked. All of these skills are part of a foundation to a great human-horse relationship. Bundy Bear had very limited understanding of any of them. In fact, he had only ever had a whip used as a weapon. This day I quickly learned just how highly sensitive he was, not only to the whip, but to me.

I knew from the time when I first got him that he needed to load into the float better than he was accustomed to doing. I needed to know that I could ask him to load whilst I stood at the bottom of the ramp, and he would walk on. Float training was one of the basic foundational training for me, as I always wanted to know that my horse would be ready to load whenever he was asked.

Different horses respond in different ways to the float. Often a horse will stop when it is shown the ramp, and refuse to walk up it. I knew form the past that sometimes horses take hours to calm down and walk on. Or if they do just walk on, they would rush off backwards, which in itself would be dangerous as they could hurt themselves or the humans around.

I travelled to shows by myself, and so I needed my horses to be well trained when I handled them on the ground. Having float training mastered where the horse walks calmly on, stands and then comes out slowly, is Safety 101 to me. I would feel safer going out by myself when I knew I could rely on the horse to be sensible. There could be emergencies like taking him to a veterinarian or away from a bushfire, or simply taking him to shows. Any time wasted trying to convince him to go on could mean time wasted on survival.

During our time together, Bundy Bear had clearly shown me he was scared of the float, the loading, the standing still, the unloading, and he rushed off backwards. At one such time, he rushed off so dramatically he hurt himself and damaged the float. All because he was afraid. He's very tall, and when he rushed back, he lifted his head and hit the roof, putting a hole through the fibreglass. So I moved this training up on my priority list.

On that particular day, I parked the float under a tree, seeking refuge from the scorching heat. It was positioned between the house and the yards. After working with Bundy Bear in the yards, I felt he was ready to begin the float training. My approach was simple, gentle, and calm, but it involved a time-consuming task of allowing the horse to stop and relax before approaching the float. I aimed to wait until his breathing slowed and his eyes softened, making it easier to guide him towards the float. I had been working on this for about thirty minutes, and I sensed he was prepared for the next step. I decided to encourage Bundy Bear to try placing a foot on the ramp, understanding that this was a scary challenge for him. Overcoming this fear was a new experience since he was accustomed to being bullied and pushed around. However, when asked to make the change, he froze. It seemed impossible for him to do it, and he showed no intention of trying. He couldn't do it and wasn't going to.

He resisted by moving his hindquarters around, moving his feet and then standing sideways to the float. I knew the best way to help him to understand me was to use the whip in the gentle way I had been doing in the yards, as an extension of my arm. While on the ground, leading my horse I would use a whip to cue the horse to step forward, and having a long whip enabled me to reach further back to tap his haunch. I knew from previous horses that when the horse is a bit lazy, just the presence of the whip is often enough to motivate it to pay more attention to your cues. So it was planned that showing him the whip, or a few gentle taps would encourage him to cross the ramp and go into the float.

I had placed a long "dressage" whip on the wheel arch of the float just in case I needed it, but from where I was standing on the ramp, I couldn't reach it. At that point, Tom walked out of the house, and I asked him to pass me the whip. He picked it up, and very quietly went to hand it to me, with the flappy bit of the whip face down, so that it wasn't threatening or couldn't accidentally hit the horse. Instantly, Bundy Bear panicked. He lifted his head, his eyes seemed to almost pop out of his skull, and the whites showed around them. He snorted and spun around, bolting off, pushing past Tom and the tree, knocking Tom to the ground, and leaving me with a rope burn on my gloved hands. I could smell his anguish as I watched his backside disappear behind the house.

He galloped past the house, jumped down a garden embankment, galloped down the fence line and onto the driveway out of sight. The front gate was open to the road, and I panicked, thinking he would be gone forever, or worse hit by a car on the road. I yelled to ask Tom if he was alright, and raced off after my horse, hoping he was also okay and not hurt. I ran in the direction of where I had last seen him, imagining the worst. Luckily the drive was long enough and he had not run away, nor been hit by a car. He had stopped just before the gate where there was a patch of green grass and stood panting. I breathed a sigh of relief and slowed down as soon as I saw him, so as not to upset him anymore with hurried movements. I slowly walked up to him, talking quietly and calmly. He stood still and allowed me to take hold of the rope. He quivered in anxiety and I stayed with him for a bit to allow him to settle. When he was ready, I walked him back to the car and float to revisit some of what we had already achieved. It took at least an hour and many tries to get him to walk onto the float without hesitation.

Eventually, over more training sessions he learnt to self-load calmly. When he was shown the float ramp, his lead rope would go over his neck, and he would walk quietly into the float. That day his reaction was not lost on me. I saw in that horse a fear that was real, a fear that truly showed what had happened to him. I vowed I would do whatever I could to help him through his fear.

Discussing the situation later with Tom, we speculated that Bundy Bear had likely encountered a man who excessively used the whip aid, resulting in his fear and defensive behaviour. I pondered whether he had been subjected to beatings by one or multiple men wielding long whips. Regardless of the specifics, it was evident that this reaction had deeply ingrained itself in my horse, and it was crucial to address it.

HAYLEY'S WISDOM

The art of learning allows us to see another perspective.

If Mr Bear was a human I would recommend he go to counselling, and gain help with his fears, and learn to release the trauma he had built up. The counselling would enable him to speak up, and share how he felt, or whatever it was he needed in order to make the pain stop.

But horses don't talk, and don't understand human, so how would that work? Regardless if they did hear voices or not, I knew I needed to take things very slowly with Mr Bear, to help him to gain trust and overcome his fear. I needed to do things in a different way. I needed to learn new skills. Skills that I could use to help Mr Bear. I trusted that my lack of experience and skill would be compensated by my patience and empathy.

I loved my horse and my husband loved his motorbike. He spent weekends waxing it, polishing it, tweaking the engine, and taking it out only in good weather. But motorcycles don't have feelings and horses do. Whilst I hadn't realised it with George, I had learnt over the few months of being with Mr Bear that horses are different, they have feelings. In the past, Bundy Bear had been "loved" by others who loved him in the same way my husband loved his motorbike. He would be fed, watered, and brushed, just as Tom would do to the motorbike – wash it, change the oil, give it fuel. Tom is a gentle person who had a mad passion for racing his motorbike, and he spends many hours in his shed twiddling the bits to make it go faster (I didn't have a clue what he was doing, but it made him happy).

There is no emotional connection, no heart-to-heart energetic connection with a bike as there is with a horse. A bike can't love you back, but when you connect in that way with a horse, it can love you back. I wanted to know the way to love Bundy Bear so that he would love me back. I needed to figure out the way he wanted to be treated and handled.

The first weekend I got Bundy Bear, I took him to my riding club. He got off the float and paced around, continually moving his legs as if he was getting ready to gallop off at any moment; his head was in the air, and he wouldn't settle. He put his nose to the wind, sniffed it and froze. His whole body started to shake, almost uncontrollably. I walked him around to try and calm the panic that I could see arising. After some time I felt he had relaxed enough to tie to the float. But he was wide eyed and on constant alert. I knew he was afraid, and this told me so much about my next moves with him. I knew a horse with that much fear was not a safe horse to ride. So for me this journey was going to take a long time. Time that he needed to gain the trust of going out again.

This experience confirmed my decision to start small, to build up his courage and feeling of safety. That meant not actually taking him out to competitions to ride him until he was ready. For the first ten months I would put him on the horse float, take him to an event, take him off the float and whilst I held him, I would let him just stand there. Initially, he would shake and quiver, and look around with a wild, open eye. The float was always filled with a wet sloppy poo, indicating he had been stressed whilst travelling to the event. Then when he was ready, when his breathing was calm, and he was able to walk, I would walk him around the event and let him eat from the green patches of grass. Sometimes he would be overwhelmed, and he would want to run, other times he would shake with fear. My aim was to get him to take those small steps, so he could find his courage, while I let him know I was there and not going to hurt him. Sometimes, I would just stand beside him as we watched whatever activity was going on around us. I would bury my face into his amazing nostrils and breathe in his scent of baked biscuits. It was so calming to me, and I think it was for him too.

Slowly he gained courage so that he could go to the event, stand, and walk around without getting all stressed.

Whilst we were making progress in some areas, I continued to be troubled by the way Bundy Bear was behaving, and his reactions and emotions. It seemed that he would come close to me, and then get angry and kick out. It was like a "push- pull" situation. He would push you away and pull you into him. I suspected he was holding onto a lot of trauma, he didn't seem happy, and yet I didn't know how to help him release what he was holding so that he could be happy.

During my research, I found out that the horse's heart is almost five times the size of my own. This huge heart gives them an incredible ability to facilitate a greater depth of connection and experience. Once I observed this, I became honest with myself and started to look at my own actions, feelings and thoughts. How I was playing out at home, at the workplace and in the horse yard. Connection to me is awareness. The horses "see" us and feel and then respond to our energy. I needed to connect to his heart.

In the time that I had been a leader, I'd worked out that the way I showed up in front of the team, affected them and their responses. If I was bad tempered, and gave short answers, then the team would reflect this back to me. If I was open and curious, then the team would open up and often become productive and innovative.

Sometimes, with Bundy, I found I needed to move with purpose for him to feel my presence. Just like when I am at work walking down a hall, and another is walking the other way with their head down totally unaware I am there, clearly on their way to somewhere important. So I move out of their way because I feel their presence, and don't wish to collide into them.

For Bundy, he had been unintentionally trained to tune humans out as they hadn't been owning their space enough for him to feel it. He needed me to make my presence known, just like when I was in the workplace.

Reflecting on my knowledge of emotional intelligence, I contemplated its essence: the capacity to comprehend one's own emotions and their impact on others. It involved the aptitude to truly grasp another person's perspective during social interactions, prioritising their needs over one's own. In contrast, individuals lacking emotional intelligence tended to treat others disrespectfully. In a professional setting, such behaviour could lead to detrimental consequences such as reduced employee engagement or a high turnover rate due to the toxic dynamics between individuals.

I wondered if that also applied to horses. Bundy Bear was showing up like an employee who had low engagement and low self-esteem. I wondered if it was because he had come from a toxic relationship with his past riders. He didn't trust humans and found it hard to connect with them in an emotionally positive way. The only way to find out was to try to put in place steps I had learned that were effective with my staff, to see if he also responded in a like manner.

I had been told by my Oma, my maternal grandmother, and also my mother, about the existence of an energy that envelops us. Since I was young, I was instilled with the belief that everything we perceive —what we see, hear, and feel—is fundamentally energy. This understanding led me to believe in the profound interconnectedness of all beings. I believed that every individual is linked through this energy, to the extent that one's thoughts could be heard by another person deeply connected to them, such as my mother or aunt. So I couldn't help but wonder: if humans can have this connection, why not horses too?

I started to discuss this with my friends, and whilst some of them thought I was going batty, I also found that there were others who felt the same way.

Once when discussing it with my friend Hayley, I mused, "so if in humans the impact of your energy affected them, I'm sure horses also can feel it and respond to that feeling too." Hayley, who also worked with energy fields agreed with me.

"Totally. Yes they can" she said. "Your energy introduces you before you even enter the room. People can subconsciously pick up on it, negative, positive, hyper, without even seeing you." She went on.

Working with my team, I noticed that the impact of my words and actions was huge. Or one small action by a team member could have a ripple effect that affected countless others. I recalled when a co-worker was being relentlessly negative and complaining all the time, and how it darkened everyone's mood and made the whole team less positive and less motivated. This started to escalate into an environment lacking in enjoyment and satisfaction. I also noticed the team started to get poor results. This vicious cycle can be destructive, and also so easily remedied. So now that I was aware of what was happening, I needed to apply the principles I was using with Bundy to myself at work.

These instances made me remember an excerpt from No Man is an Island, a poem by John Donne, which I had studied in school.

No man is an island,
Entire of itself,
Every man is a piece of the continent,
A part of the main.
If a clod be washed away by the sea,
Europe is the less.
As well as if a promontory were.
As well as if a manor of thy friend's
Or of thine own were.
Any man's death diminishes me,
Because I am involved in mankind,
And therefore never send to know for whom the bell tolls;
It tolls for thee.

What happens to one person, happens to us all. There is connection between all humankind, and connection is better than isolation. Just like a horse, connection is important and what happens to one, happens to them all.

From years of trying, I'd worked out that any time I tried to improve myself, or break a habit, it needed to come from inside of me, and then it could move outside into new behaviours and habits. I recalled the time Tom told me I was changing, for the better, and how hard it had been for me to take it in. Yet as I sat with it, I realised it was true; everything he said, and it was that processing that helped me. In order to help Bundy Bear make a shift in his behaviours I needed to work on myself. I needed time to observe, and then process things. So with this new insight I tried positivity. From years of experience, I knew it could spread just as quickly and contagiously as negativity.

I started to show up in the stable and anywhere Bundy Bear was, as optimistic, goal-oriented, and quietly confident. I tried to notice if I was being too pushy, or wanting something instantly. I still got caught out and would realise well afterwards, yet I was aware of my habits now, and I had a choice to make the change. I knew the more patience I had, the easier it would be for him to change. Day after day I would show up in that way, and I believed it made a difference to my horse. After some time I could see it had inspired Bundy Bear to do the same and it was making a big change in his demeanour..

This awareness had me seeing all sorts of habits I had befriended. An area I had noticed was negative responses to the world around me. Once I became aware and started changing my usual negative responses into more positive ones, things around me started to change. People were respecting me more, and asking for my opinion.

Now I'm not perfect; in fact sometimes I get grumpy - seriously, really angry - and for no reason. So my relationship with Tom had been pushed to its limits and it seemed I was hell-bent on ruining my marriage. I would come home from the office carrying all the weight of the office politics, and then rather than giving a warm smile and a kiss, I'd dump all that junk and bad mood straight onto poor Tom. We had a rule where we needed to kiss and make up before we went to bed, but sometimes that sucked. So some nights I'd storm off, and just hide in the bedroom. Then the next morning, I'd get up and would be even angrier with him.

"Why didn't he just apologise?' I said to myself one morning after a bad night. I stormed out of the door, and stomped my way to the yards. When I got there, all the horses were looking up at me, with big open eyes. It was as if they all said in unison, "Holy shit, watch out she's in a mood!" I stopped and thought about that. Yep! I sure was.

The horses were up in the stables waiting for some food. As I entered they stood and looked at me, all of them, ears pricked and on edge. They were on alert for danger. From me. The stables and yards were connected and I always had given the horses the freedom to move around in the whole space in the evening. Suddenly Bundy bolted out of the stable door into the yards and trotted to the furthest corner of the yard. He stopped and turned to stare at me, his head high and alert.

OK, I thought, this is my time to make a choice. A choice of how I want to react. I can be grumpy and scare the shit out of the horses, or I can pull my head in and act like an adult. I looked at the horses, and knew there really was no choice; I had to be an adult.

After I had finished feeding and preparing the horses for the night I walked quietly back into the house. "I'm sorry" I said to Tom when he appeared in the kitchen "I'm being a shit, and for that I apologise" he tried to hide his shock, but I noticed.

I learnt to stop and listen, becoming conscious of the reactions I was triggering, and then making adjustments accordingly. Interestingly, I soon realised that this newfound practice of attentive listening and awareness was gradually becoming a new norm for me in all aspects of my life. It positively impacted my team at work, as well as my interactions with my horses and my home life. In the past, it was easy for me to let bad news or unfavourable outcomes deeply affect me. I could become snappy, and a single negative event had the power to ruin my entire day if I allowed it to. However, my new habits with my horse had heightened my awareness of my own reactions and extended to how I interacted with my team. I fostered new habits and cultivated a fresh way of being.

The whole process of thinking about how I felt, and then taking time to process the information before I continued was a game changer. It made me more confident in front of my team, and the team responded accordingly. It literally made my life a better place! It was hard, and took effort, but it paid off big time.

I had created a ripple effect that brought more joy and fulfilment into the lives of my team, my friends, my family, and of course, my horse.

One of the practices I commenced during that time was to write down three things I was grateful for each day. I had read some research that discussed how this is one of the easiest ways to make yourself happy. I started sharing these things with my husband every night. Remarkably, it also made a difference in his outlook. It was simple enough, and something we could do together, making a bigger impact. I was grateful for things at work, and in my personal life. The subjects varied and they didn't have to be just horse or work related; they could be things like:

- A team member who made an effort.
- Bundy Bear making an improvement.
- Me getting out of bed happy
- A project going well.
- A thank you received from someone.

Once we started, this practice made a huge impact on our lives. It has been helpful for both of our mental health, my working relationships and productivity. It is something that I am not willing to give up any time soon.

COURAGE

To lose courage is to become stuck.
To gain courage is to grow into your best self.

For Bundy Bear, fear, like many emotions, was closely linked to his survival. There were actions, like taking him to shows and being hit with a whip, where his survival was threatened and this would cause a surge of adrenaline which meant that he would go into a 'fight' or 'flight' mode. Physically, he would exhibit signs such as sweating, widened eyes, readiness to gallop or even trembling.

Not long after I got him, I discussed this reaction with my friend, Hayley over a coffee one day. Hayley was someone who had been around horses most of her life, but she no longer rode. She was someone who thought in a way that I resonated with, and for that, I liked her and our conversations. I knew Bundy was showing signs of fear, and yet I wanted him to have his courage to shine again. I wanted him to be able to feel the fear, and then for him to show courage and use that to be able to manage and overcome it, so that it didn't stop him from taking action.

As I met up with her, I noticed her outfit. Hayley was an amazing dresser, always looking like she was out for a job interview. I noted her beautiful turquoise top with the gold trim, and white Capri pants. She smelled divine, like a bouquet of roses and something more earthy, more sensual and intoxicating.

"Are you going somewhere nice after this?" I asked as I sat down. "You smell awesome, by the way – that perfume is stunning"

"I've just been to the bank, the nail salon, and now coffee with you" she smiled back.

I looked down at Hayley's immaculate pink nails with gold stars, each looking beautifully manicured, and then across on my own, cut short because of my work with horses and dirt under them. I folded them into my palms. I glanced down at the clothes I had hastily thrown on before I left. Oh dear I thought, I looked and smelled as if I had just left the stable yard.

"I should have made an effort this morning," I berated myself. Even though I'd come straight from the yard, and knew that horses don't judge me based on my appearance, I was now judging myself because of the way I had dressed. I ploughed on.

"What's 'courage' to you?" I asked Hayley, feeling out of sorts as I sat next to her shiny presence. It seemed I was drawing on all of my courage to even be at the same table.

"That's like when I have the confidence to walk into a room full of executives," she replied.

As we sat at the table I picked up my phone and did a search for the definition of courage. The dictionary definition on my screen read,

"Courage - the quality of mind or spirit that enables a person to face difficulty, danger, pain, etc., without fear."

I so needed that courage now and I opened my hands without worrying about how my nails looked, to prove I could do it.

"So how do you tell a horse he needs to overcome the fear in his mind? Or even lead a horse you are not communicating with?" I asked my friend. "I am not sure I want him to NOT have fear when facing these situations. In fact, I think I want him to demonstrate courage when he is fearful and proceed despite his fear."

"It's all about the trust of the partnership; the rider and the horse and his wellbeing," Hayley replied and then went on "I know when I was working with my horses I spent the first part of our relationship building trust. When I did that well, we could do anything together. That's what you are looking for here with Bundy"

"Ahh...," he feels scared, anxious and uncomfortable in relationships. "That is now making sense; He finds it hard to connect emotionally," I said.

"Yes," said Hayley thoughtfully. "What you'll find is when he was exposed to miscommunication, he became sullen, shut down, and even got angry. Some horses have learned there is no point in making an effort, so they shut down. They must be thinking there is no point in trying to communicate with a species that doesn't take an interest in them, in listening or in seeing the horse's perceptions. I had a horse just like him. Harmony was her name, a beautiful horse in the end, but not when we got her. She was rude, and angry and aggressive. It took me months, maybe years of working slowly with her."

"Mmm," came my response as I placed my fingers on my cheek, thinking about what she had just said, and how Bundy certainly did react that way. Oh dear, the poor soul.

"And now you have the task of getting him to see that life doesn't have to be like that," said Hayley.

"OK," said I, putting my coffee cup down, and considering all the possibilities, with no clue as to how I would start this. "And how do you think I do that?" I voiced my thoughts out loud. "If he was a member of my team I would have a quiet chat with him, ask him what's going on, or in a bad case I'd recommend the company psychologist for support. I can't do either with a horse."

"Yes, you can," replied Hayley, dissecting the small slice of cake we had decided to share, with her fork. "He might be a horse but he still listens, and still wants to be connected, just as we humans do. You might just have to approach it in a different way."

"What you need to do is allow him to take small steps towards your goal, and show him that he can do it. Give him the confidence he is doing well, and offer small treats to reward his progress. This will allow him to push past those emotions and maybe even the voices he has in his head." added Hayley.

"You really think he has voices in his head?" I asked before placing the last mouthful of cake on my fork and finishing the slice.

"I do, yes," said Hayley before taking a sip of her coffee, and continuing, "that and through body language. He'll immediately pick up on your emotions and notice the most subtle movements from you. So you have to be really mindful of that."

Hayley continued, "if you want to be able to tell him that he doesn't have to be scared, you will need to do it by remaining calm yourself and not getting stressed."

"You're right, we don't want to let those voices get any bigger, so that he is feeding his fear. I need to be able to support him, and show him a way to have the courage to take small steps. OK. I can do this," I replied.

I wanted to draw upon his self-worth and allow him to express himself. It took time, and lots of courage, on both our parts to build up the trust. His courage would waiver as different situations arose. He would be strong one day, and then not so much the next.

As I learned to work with my horse, I ultimately began to learn about myself.

My journey was really exciting for me, and even though I was intuitive, and an animal lover, I've always possessed a strong intuition and a deep love for animals. When I was younger, I was a loner, which allowed me to observe and absorb the world around me. This enabled me to attune myself to people's energy and truly listen to them.

However, as I grew into adulthood, I had unconsciously abandoned this practice of attentive listening. I started believing that I needed to respond immediately in order to fit in or appear like a remarkable leader, at least that's what I thought at the time. This change in behaviour was a learned response, likely influenced by societal expectations or my own misguided perception of what constituted effective leadership.

Now, I recognise the importance of reconnecting with my intuitive abilities and reclaiming the art of listening. True leadership and genuine connection arise from understanding and engaging with others on a deeper level. I now understand that being a great leader involves more than just quick responses—it requires empathetic understanding and thoughtful communication.

Once again, I was learning to tune into animals. I wanted that ability to come back, the one that allowed me to listen with an open heart so that I could see so much more, and gain an understanding I never had. I knew it was time to make my change to help my horse.

With this in mind, I wanted to let Bundy Bear realise that by taking small steps, where he wasn't harmed, he could win. When it was repeated often enough he would begin to see it as "normal" and then I could move to the next step to help him. Just like a muscle, the more I practised expanding his courage, the stronger it would grow. So with practice and consistent effort, I started working with Bundy Bear to increase his courage muscle.

Every major goal was broken down into small steps. I took him to shows just to walk him around and show him that he wasn't going to be beaten or traumatised; I created more small steps for him. His life became full of small steps. Steps like putting the saddle on, and then taking it off, and when he stood calmly without fidgeting, I would put him away as a reward. Then repeating this for three or four days in a row. Each day, I would consider how he responded, and maybe add a new task for him, like walking with the saddle on, and then taking it off. Some days he would get treats, other days he would just get the relief of being put back in his paddock with his friends. Whilst it was slow going, I was happy to take the time.

I was driven by the goal of having this beautiful horse show his true self one day, and therefore he could take whatever time it took for him to heal and grow. And with this practice of 'small steps' I was able to get on and ride him and attend dressage lessons within six months of getting him. I knew, just like building a house, he needed a strong foundation to support him in his journey of life.

Later that day as I walked back into the house, I reflected upon the conversation with Hayley, and how Bundy had been reacting.

When Tom appeared, he handed me a glass of wine and I said, "You know, when we think of courageous people in our lives, we might think of heroic figures, maybe ones from movies or comic books."

I walked outside to our new decking area beckoning Tom to follow. As he sat down with a bowl of nuts and his beer, I continued "Having courage is something different to what we know from our schooling and films; it isn't about being the person at the front of the army, leading the charge and taking the brunt of any enemy attacks; it's more about being aware of the voices in your head, and thanking them, then taking those small steps to create new and more positive habits."

"Yes," said Tom, and waited.

"Well, I think Bundy is learning the art of being courageous. I think over time it was taken out of him, and now I want to help him get it back"

"That's awesome news, darling," came his reply. "That horse is so lucky to have you in his life."

"I think it's me who is the winner. I'm learning so much from him. Small steps." I said contemplatively.

Tom said, "I think of courage as being able to push through barriers that you are faced with, to be spontaneous and genuine, and to take big steps into the unknown. I know when I have been able to challenge my status quo, and step into the unknown to learn and grow, it has come being able to have the courage to take that first step. In the past, I accepted the norms I was surrounded by, what was shared through my family, and friends, and it kept me small. Yet when I have had the courage to move away from them, I was able to really grow."

"You know," I said thinking about courageous people I knew at work "When you lead with courage you inspire courage and others love to follow that courage."

"Yes, my point exactly," said Tom beaming.

"And that leads to communication," I said.

"What do you mean?" he asked

"Well," I started, "being authentically courageous is about being able to speak your truth without disclosing every single thought and feeling you have."

"Huh! If only people would take the time to stop, ask questions, be quiet, and listen, we would probably get better, more lasting results," said Tom.

"Yes, and having the ability to sit silently while others ask for advice and guide them to the answers is also key," I said thinking of some fellow workers.

"We don't learn this in school, and yet it is so important," Tom replied.

"I often find myself wishing that schools taught a 'Life Basics 101' course. It would cover essential skills like effective communication, which goes beyond simply providing answers. Instead, it would emphasise the importance of allowing people the space to think and figure things out on their own," I remarked, taking a sip of my wine and realising that my glass was empty.

"Those are definitely important strengths for anyone to have," said Tom.

"That's what I've been trying to do with Bundy," I said.

"Brilliant, and it sounds like what you are doing must be working." Tom replied.

"I'm learning that when I'm faced with a problem, and to understand it deeper, I need to give the problem some time. Just as I was doing when working with Mr Bear; time and curiosity are key to my success," I said. "Being quiet inside allows me to be more present and in the moment, which is how I am able to observe the subtleties of his language. When I stopped and listened, I found he had an impressive talent for getting his point across."

"Like what?" asked Tom.

I stopped twiddling the glass I was holding, and pondered. "Well," I said, "Normally when I go into the stables I will be really busy. Busy preparing the feeds, or grooming him, or even tacking him up. But when I slow that pace down, and really think about stopping and listening, I see so much more. Just yesterday, I arrived and Bundy was in his stable, so rather than bustling off to get his tack and ride him as I was planning on doing, I just stopped and stood. We stood for a minute or so, and then he looked at me, really looked. I felt at that moment that he wanted to connect with me on the ground and not be ridden. I'm not sure how he said it, but I felt it.

Anyway I decided I would do some ground work and took him out to the yard. We had the best session together, and I felt like he really wanted to be there with me. I felt like he was sharing his wisdom from his heart. It really was the most amazing moment. It seemed he was opening up to me, our bond is getting stronger and stronger AND the best part was - it was exactly what I needed at the time. I had been feeling icky about a situation at work, and it was bubbling away in my head. After that session with Bundy the bubbles had totally dissolved. There are many other times I'm seeing this now, but I won't bore you with them all."

"That's great news!" Tom said with a huge smile across his face. I could see how excited he was.

I was so pleased with his response, it was like he was urging me on. So I continued, "He opens up to me totally and I love the slowness of the pace, it just builds upon that connection and bond. I am so proud and happy that we don't listen to the many people who say we are not going fast enough. This is my horse, my journey, and we do it our way."

I was clearly seeing that establishing ways to be "present" with my horse allowed me to see his equine language, and to share with me insights through mirroring back what I needed to know at that time. These sessions on the ground were beneficial for both of us. He was gaining confidence in me and the questions I asked. He then could apply that knowledge when I was in the saddle. It was about listening to the pace he needed, and then being deliberately slow enough to meet his need and so that he could understand.

Once I realised what was happening, I considered whether these skills would be beneficial in other parts of my life as well. I knew my leadership skills needed work, and so I started practising sitting and listening to others, and then giving myself time to digest and process my learnings. At first, it was challenging for me because I had become accustomed to quickly responding to their questions without taking time to reflect. This often led to giving incorrect answers or misunderstanding the situation entirely.

The act of sitting still, listening, and waiting required a significant effort on my part. There were moments when I felt self-conscious about waiting and my mind eagerly wanted to jump in and respond. To overcome this, I had to genuinely believe in the importance of pausing. During these instances, I started telling myself, "Think like Bundy. Be Bundy." These thoughts helped me create that necessary space and take the time to pause and reflect.

Over time I started to see the results. It impacted my personal friends, and my work colleagues. I found that the point of seeking to understand wasn't just to allow others to feel heard and to inspire trust; it was also to demonstrate that I "got" the person I was talking to. I found that I began to understand perspectives different from my own, and this in turn allowed me to be more inclusive, perceptive, and empathetic. It also started a process of others sharing more with me.

What I realised was, over time I was gaining the courage to just 'be', something that would have scared me prior to this point. This stillness of 'being' was very cathartic and it was increasing my courage to experiment with other aspects in my life. One of my best tactics was to bury my face on the side of his nose and breathe deep. Breathe in that lightly herbed biscuit smell, like they had just come out of the oven. It was heaven and extremely liberating.

So whilst I was helping Bundy with his courage, and reducing his stress, I also was gaining the same insights. For me too, the journey was huge. There were times when I really needed to connect to someone and ask their help, or guidance. After I'd worked him my mind would race with questions like, "Was it too much for him, was it too soft?"

When I had paid instructors to come out and coach us, I felt they were intent only on imparting their knowledge, and not listening to what was happening for us. So it was difficult to discuss with them.

Tom was a good listener, but he wasn't a horse rider, so he could only support me from his perspective.

"Am I giving him a reason to learn bad habits, or am I working on building his trust?" I would ask, and Tom would give me a non-committal "I don't know" or "does it feel too much? Has he reacted?"

I hardly ever had someone watching me who I trusted. So I would reach out and find someone to help me, or listen to me. Sometimes that person was a horse person and other times they were professional mentors. It was during these times that I realised I needed to work on my own reflection processes.

If I was honest with myself, I had to confront my courage on a daily basis. Some days, it felt like an unstoppable force, empowering me to tackle anything that came my way. But then, there were those days when it seemed to vanish, leaving me longing to hide behind my computer screen, avoiding any human interaction.

In those challenging moments, when I needed to summon my courage, whether to challenge the status quo, embrace change, or step outside of the expected norms, it was a genuine struggle. Yet, there were instances when I witnessed the positive impact of a small change I had made, and the feeling was exhilarating. It was during this period of working with my horse that I began to exercise and strengthen my courage, gradually reshaping my mindset to recognise my own unique brand of courage.

Learning is just the beginning. I was conscious that as my confidence grew from communicating with my horse, team, and husband, that I shouldn't lose sight of the fact that there will always be more learning to do. Having this kind of confidence didn't mean I knew everything there was to know, rather the courage to find ways to move forward based on what I did know. I felt empowered to try new things, grow, and learn from the experience.

Throughout this process, I not only built my own confidence and belief in my abilities, but I also witnessed Bundy's confidence growing day by day. I realised that I couldn't force him to be confident; instead, it was through creating a comfortable environment for him that he began to develop confidence on his own.

Slowing down became my new normal, and interestingly, it accelerated his ability to grasp the new way of being. As his learning progressed, I gradually expanded his enhanced confidence, equipping him to handle challenging situations that arise in his everyday life. With this newfound confidence and by taking small steps, he became unfazed by anything, even if it was outside his comfort zone.

My ability to exude a quiet, confident assertiveness translated into a sense of "calm" with the horses. It conveyed the message that "all is well" and fostered a mutual trust between us.

Just as I communicated with words, I also became aware of the way I communicated with my physical self and behaviour through working with Bundy. Standing tall with a core strength, walking with pride, and speaking with intention are all ways I could change what happened in the yards, and ways that helped my inner confidence. Just as it worked in the yards, it also worked when I was talking to others, at work or at home.

SELF AWARENESS

I am responsible for my life, my feelings, my growth and for all the results I get.

One day it dawned on me that when I was stressed, Bundy Bear would stress even more. When I was calm and in control, Bundy Bear was able to handle the situation in a better way. I came to see that his reactions were a reflection of my feelings. I needed to become more self-aware.

If I walked to the yard in a funk of unconscious heightened emotion, and went to catch him, he'd shy and turn and gallop off. If I was aware of my emotional state, and brought myself into a relaxed state I could walk straight up to him. Having self-awareness meant that I needed to check in with my body on a regular basis so that I could really feel and understand my emotions. My feelings in my body guided me to knowing my emotions better. When I felt a specific body response I could reflect, to see what emotions were happening at the time and what I needed to do to best support Bundy.

This reflection allowed me to decide how I wanted to react to a situation.

In his dark days Bundy Bear had shut down because he associated certain events with pain and became cautious and anxious over new experiences. He felt he was unworthy, and he only knew pain, fear, and anger. He did as he was told, yet was in constant fear of pain. Any feedback he received was always negative, and it seemed it didn't matter what he did as his handlers assumed he deserved a whipping. His fear kept him alive and safe, but he was anxious for what could come next. He would try to gallop away from danger, to gallop away from the whip being wielded at him, and he would kick out with his legs to win his own survival. He was a big horse so he was quite dangerous when he was overcome with anxiety. His body needed reconditioning and his mind needed to be settled, so that he could feel confident in the new steps he was taking.

Standing beside him, I worked on calming his mind, and allowing him to take courageous steps in a different direction. A direction where no pain existed, only love and boundaries.

After owning him for around four months I tried riding him. Standing next to this horse I often felt slightly dwarfed, but sitting on his back I would feel nothing short of god-like. It was this feeling that kept the dream of riding him in competitions and winning prizes for what he could achieve.–He had already shown me he knew how to buck and that he had ways to try to dislodge a rider, so it took many more months of getting him to stop trying to dislodge me, slow down and process his own courage before he was a safe horse to ride.

I worked with Bundy Bear consistently for about a year trying to establish a communication of trust between us. I allowed him to experience being ridden without the pain that he had always known, without being whipped, or pulled in the mouth. Together we built a bond that was based on mutual trust. He learned to trust me, and just enjoy being with me. It was about building his trust slowly and carefully. It also was about building his courage to communicate and be heard, rather than being shut down.

I wanted him to realise he was worthy, unique, and a beautiful soul. Building that solid foundation was extremely important, so when he became unnerved or anxious he knew he had a safe base to go back to.

There were times when I needed an expert to come and help me, as I couldn't see what was being presented. I had an amazing animal body worker who would come and "feel" into the horse, sense their emotions and their muscles. I would bring her out every few weeks, to help me to understand what was happening with Bundy. I was shown by her one day how he had been clenching his teeth, and where the muscles had built up. She explained to me how this build up was where he was holding his fears which in turn was affecting his body. Ultimately I wanted him to be softer all over his body, so that he could become a nimble athlete.

The body worker and I devised a plan. During the riding training I was steadily aiming for a softer jaw, so that we could find more looseness and straightness. When I felt he was softer in the jaw, I knew he was releasing his fears.

Working on his body and with his body worker also allowed me to see how he reacted to different aids when riding. Sometimes I found that it was easier for Bundy Bear to produce lateral work, than for him to work forwards and cover the ground. I was becoming aware of the physical restrictions he had in his body shape.

At times progress seemed painfully slow, with a few settled and attentive sessions, then for some reason Bundy Bear would show evasion and inattentive behaviour. I was keen to gain his focus during work, which took both diplomacy and tact, while trying to maintain the calm energy in his mind. When he was inattentive or shying at everything that was or wasn't there, I would become frustrated. If at this point I showed this frustration as anger or being demanding, where he would feel pressured into doing something he wasn't ready to do, then the trust that had been built up would quickly disappear.

He had shown me that, in the past with previous riders, he had complied when pressure was put on him, yet that caused him to lose sight of joy and freedom. Under this pressure he learnt to clench his jaw and produce stiff and stilted paces. So it was my intent to not put that kind of pressure on him, while still teaching him to do what I needed him to do. It was damn hard.

One day whilst riding him, I patted him on the neck, telling him he was a good boy for something small he had done. Bundy Bear stopped still, turned his head and looked at me with his left eye, as though asking, "Are you for real? Did you just say I was good?" I repeated the pat and the compliment out aloud, just to make sure that he heard and understood. He responded with a deep sigh. A sigh that brought tears to my eyes as I realised he has told me he was so happy to have received that gentle pat. A pat of encouragement, to say well done. Not a bark demanding not enough, or do more!

From that point on, I knew a pat was really special for him. It became the one thing that could be easily applied, and would help him in so many situations.

I started to question, who in my life needed gratitude or a simple thank you. "I'm being Bundy by saying 'thank you' so that it can have positive effects on my health and the well-being of others," I told Tom

"Amanda," he said "So often I forget to say thank you because favours seem normal to me."

"I know right, and then we just take it as normal, and the person never knows if they did well or not," I replied. "You aren't alone, and isn't it a sad state of being human? When someone does something good that has helped us or the team out, it seems expected and generally doesn't seem to require a thank you. No wonder people in the workplace are disgruntled"

"That is a very sad state of being human, and it also appears to be that way when humans interact with horses," Tom said

"It's time for me to start recognising the efforts of others, and thanking them," I said.

"Be Bundy," said Tom.

"Exactly," I replied. "I'm going to practice on humans, just as I do on horse, to say it out loud and to see a smile on somebody's face, and to feel good about doing it. No matter how small the action, people will be thankful, and feel validated."

A relationship with a horse is similar to any friendship. Tom was grateful for the work I was doing on Bundy and "Being Bundy" as he put it. He could see the changes in me, even if I couldn't myself.

Working with a horse is perhaps more exaggerated than with a friend, and it is a great place to learn, because a horse gives instant feedback. Working diligently on his recovery program I had learnt ways to build his trust, rather than trigger his trauma response. And just like any friendship, if one or the other were to get argumentative, angry or even become abusive, then the trust would be gone, and I would need to start to build up that trust again. Not that I was going to be aggressive with him, but there were times when I needed to stand my ground and tell him he couldn't walk over me, so to speak.

So the process was not linear. It was more like a set of stairs where you go up a couple of flights and then go back down one, but never down as far as the bottom. So that over time the foundation of trust was building up.

For humans, when they've had a trauma, there is an internal need to feel safe and cared for. I had read that trauma can be so overwhelming that it creates an internal chaos and this in turn distorts the person's ability to gauge realistic offers. In this situation, the human has an altered view of what they want. When I thought about this I wondered if this was what was happening when I was working with Bundy Bear. Some days I found that there was a fine line to balance the relationship, and build trust.

This process that I considered to be backwards and forwards meant that I was constantly questioning myself, and my ability to manage helping Bundy Bear. When working Bundy there were times when I knew I had got the right formula, and other times when I wondered what was going on. I would ask him a question and sometimes it would be a big response, and other times it was small and, just like Goldilocks, sometimes it would be 'just right'. What I did to get those responses though was a mystery to me.

Just as I had to work on courage, I also had to work on feeling my fear of not being a "good rider" as part of my self-awareness when around Bundy Bear. I was hell bent on making sure I provided the best possible opportunity for my horse. Even if this meant doing something when no one else believed in what I was doing, and would tell me so. I knew I was doing the right thing. My inner voice would be saying "go for it – you have to do this" but outwardly there would be a different storyline happening.

A story where others would be voicing their opinions, and telling how it had to done. Some horsey people just keep going on and on until you say 'yes I will do it" whatever "it" is. I would find myself smiling back at these well-meaning others saying, "Oh you know, maybe I can think about it, maybe it's not the right thing for my horse". Inwardly I'm thinking, "not a chance! Lady".

When I embarked on the journey of approaching horses in a more holistic manner, my unconventional thinking often drew comments from others suggesting what they believed I should do instead. It felt both daunting and exhilarating to have the opportunity to support horses in a different way than the traditional methods.

Having the courage to embrace my true self allowed the universe to present me with unexpected gifts. This newfound authenticity not only transformed my interactions with horses but also had a ripple effect in other areas of my life. The way I approached horses and tailored my assistance to their unique personalities influenced how I interacted with people as well.

It took a lot of time and much soul searching to get to this point. I recalled a time at the beginning of my journey with Bundy Bear when I had taken him to a dressage clinic held at one of the local rider's property. There were about ten ladies from the dressage club that I belonged to and we had a leading international dressage instructor taking the lessons.

As it was a dressage club event, I took time to prepare and to look the part. I had gone out and bought myself some new basic clothing especially for the clinic, and I was feeling pretty good as I took my horse off the float. I felt comfortable in my new top, waist coat and jodhpurs. My riding boots were clean and I had washed my hairy pony so that whilst he was long haired, he was clean and his white mane shone.

At lunchtime, we all sat around a wooden table in the shade of a tree out by the dressage arena. Whilst the air was cool, the sun was gliding in and out behind clouds, and the effort of riding kept everyone warm, so the shade provided some relief. The horses were all comfortably tied to the floats, some with smart rugs on and all eating from their hay bags. Everyone had brought their own lunches and it seemed the protocol was to share it around the table. The host had brought out some large plates, and these were piled high with grapes, and cheeses, and olives and dips. It was a magical day for me, everything a horse person could dream of. I thought, this is what I've missed; being in the company of like-minded souls. Little did I actually know!

"You know," said one of the immaculately dressed ladies on the far side of the table. She was dressed in the latest fashion, a steel blue riding polo shirt with gold embroidered emblem. I looked up at her and remembered how earlier I had been in awe of her matching saddlecloth, bonnet and bandages on her horse. In fact, the fashion on all of the horses was astounding, there was bling where I had no idea bling could go. I was about to ask her where she shopped, but stopped myself, and waited to hear what words of wisdom she had to share with whomever she was talking to.

"You shouldn't have your horse barefoot, it is dangerous." I looked around to see who she was talking to, and realised it was me.

"Sorry, are you talking to me?" I asked incredulously.

"Well they need to have the shoes on so they are safe, it supports them…" she stated. I was curious to hear what else others said, so I smiled and continued eating the offerings on my plate. It seemed the smile was enough, but it appeared they had all been talking about me behind my back. Determined to have their say, they all told me how wrong I was in having my horse barefoot.

I watched the ladies with my mouth closed (at least I'd learnt that skill).

But I was getting upset and my hands started to shake. I placed my hands, one around my bottle of water, the other flat, on the table to steady them so no one would see that they were shaking. The ladies continued and I heard the whole shebang from everyone around the gathering.

"Horseshoes aid in the durability of the hoof on all working horses. They simply MUST be worn."

"You can't ride dressage on a horse with no shoes."

"The shoes support and provide protection…"

"If you wish to be successful, you can't possibly ride him barefoot," stated the instructor.

"They provide protection on hard rocky footing and traction."

They went on and on.

I tried to respond, to back up my reasoning, but it didn't work. They kept talking *at* me, rather than *to* me, and I felt like I was under a microscope. It seemed to me they were picking everything I did to bits. My thoughts seemed jumbled, and I struggled to articulate myself clearly. Every time I spoke, it felt as if I was stumbling over my words, leaving me sounding clueless. It was frustrating because nobody seemed to listen or even make an effort to understand what I was trying to say. The overwhelming sensation of being talked at without anyone asking for my perspective stirred up a whirlwind of emotions within me, leading me to eventually give up on trying to make them understand.

My self-confidence took a significant blow, leaving me feeling completely shaken and uncertain of myself.

Yet deep down I still believed in what I had read about the barefoot horse, the benefits it had brought George, and how Bundy Bear loved being barefoot, whether they heard me or not, I was determined to continue. So I remained on what seemed to be my solo journey.

This incident was not alone, it just seemed horsey people had a way of denting self-confidence. For whatever reason, they would become opinionated, often loud, and overbearing and believed wholeheartedly that their opinion should be followed by everyone. There were many times at that club where I felt steamrolled by others. As well as the foot issue, I would be told that in dressage you can't ride a coloured horse, or no don't do that, this is better, or that I needed to ride in a certain saddle (even though the dressage rules don't mention it), or I should feed my horse this feed, and a hundred other opinionated instructions.

"Whilst the advice might've been coming from a good place, it got to me, when it appeared that everything I did was wrong, or every horse I liked was ugly, or the way I held my reins was slightly different. These freely given opinions, which they believed were facts, brought on my insecurities. It was interesting though that often the loudest rider to state their opinion had the worst horse. They spouted their horsemanship knowledge at every turn, yet it was their horse that would cause the biggest drama when out, or it would bite, or would dig massive holes under the float as it was tied there. Realising this, I smiled to myself and kept going on my own journey of discovery to help my horse in the best way I could. To me the art of horsemanship was about tuning into the horse so that I could master my thoughts, and body movements to affect their behaviour. Not to tie the horse down and force it to comply, rather allow them to tune into me and I with them. I knew the greatest change was going to come when I was being responsible for my own behaviour.

The path with this incredible horse and my holistic thinking, meant that Bundy Bear kept me in touch with who I was, and continually acknowledged my fear. I was learning to be open and see my own truth, and in return he taught me and helped me to find a means of empowerment. I found that I couldn't hide from the fear, rather when I acknowledged it I would say to myself, 'well it's OK to feel nervous'. And then a strange thing would happen: once the fear was acknowledged and recognised for what it was, much of the worry and fear dissolved.

In this way, I was able to take responsibility for my actions and then find a way to change the situation before it destroyed my self-confidence.

This is what I did

I made a list of every fear that I had.

In a notebook or journal, whatever I had at the time, I would record a list of all the fears I had just experienced. This was a private list, just for me, so I could write whatever I wanted.

As I wrote down these fears, I would note how they made me feel.

I'd make note of the fears that gave me the strongest feeling, so I knew these were the ones to work on. I knew that I was seeking to find which fears are healthy and which were holding me back from fully participating in my life.

After writing them down I would circle the ones that were opportunities for growth, and healing.

I would place a star alongside the goals that felt important, yet scared me.

And most important of all, I knew that no matter how uncomfortable I felt, by writing this list down I was committing to taking action on my fears.

Describing my feelings and fears allowed me to reduce the attachment to it and helped reduce the emotional negative responses.

VOICING MY FEARS

Fear can be so restrictive, yet when voiced they dissipate.
We are told not to voice them, to hide them, to stop them.
Yet when they are voiced they become small.

On Thursday evening at school, I walked in to the room with some classmates. We were chatting about the weekend and I found myself reflecting about my horse. "Voicing your fear doesn't make you weak — it makes you brave. The more you get into the habit of choosing to voice your fear, the more you walk towards becoming unstoppable." I said, knowing this was my truth.

Charlie piped up and said "Have the courage to change your habits. Make a tiny change regularly to experience something unfamiliar."

"Oh I like that," I said "Thanks," writing it in my notebook for future reference.

During that whole class, as the lecturer went on about his prophecies, I thought about the habits I have, the good, the bad, and what I needed to change.

My life is full of tiny habits, especially ones I am not aware of. And these habits, even the ones I am not aware of, tend to define me. I wracked my brain to recall what I had read, or been told about habits. I knew habits are formed or broken by repetition. I wanted to Google more, but stayed acting like I was interested in the class, and wrote down a note to read more after class.

"Charlie," I asked as we left later that evening, "what do you know about habits?"

"They are what we repeatedly do and think. The person we are today is essentially the sum of your habits," he said.

"I know I do pretty dumb things sometimes," I said. " I wondered if I'll ever learn my lesson."

"Huh! That's funny. I do the same. I was once told by a professor that there is power in consistency. I think that means if you are consistently creating new habits, you will succeed" Charlie said.

"Or, if you consistently do dumb things, then you stay stuck." I said walking down the steps to the car park.

"I guess now you know you're doing them, you have a choice," Charlie laughed and beeped his car alarm off.

"Okay, I get your point. Thanks for the chat Charlie, have a great night," I called back from my car.

"Will do, see you next week," I heard his say as I opened my car door and threw my books on the back seat.

I smiled and reversed out of the car park for the drive home; thinking about my habits and being aware of doing dumb things. "Why did I even say that to him?" I asked myself in the darkness of the car. "Do I do dumb things? Maybe they are some of my habits." I thought back in response.

"Be Bundy," I said to the darkened car and road ahead "Be aware and make conscious choices"

So for me to change my habits I needed to make a conscious choice to turn off the auto-pilot, to look the habits in the eye and change the ones that needed to be changed.

The first step for me was probably the hardest. I had to become conscious of my routines, my thinking and reactions that had created the life I had now. Only then could I make a change. So I started small.

I made it fun and I would experiment with making very small

changes to see what it was like to step out of my routines. I tried brushing my teeth with the opposite hand, packing a different lunch, or finding a new route to the office for three days in a row. These small changes would take me out of my comfortable routine and allow me to practice experiencing discomfort without taking any real risk. From here I would build upon what I knew.

WE ARE UNIQUE

Outward change comes after we change from within.

When Bundy Bear first came to live with me he didn't speak his mind. He tried to hide, to keep himself safe. Yet, I knew that his opinion mattered. It mattered to me how he was feeling, and how his emotions were affecting him. His thoughts and feelings were just as valid as any human's, and deserved to be heard.

Just like in my life, there were times when I kept myself small and didn't say anything, and other times I knew I deserved to have a say. It was the same with Bundy. When people tried to convince me that my viewpoint was wrong, I learnt to recognise this. I learnt to accept my own thoughts and beliefs that were true to me, and may be different from those of others. And that was okay. I wanted to instil this knowledge in Bundy. That it was okay to be different.

My strength with Bundy, my team and family lay in the recognition and acceptance that I am unique, just as Bundy Bear is. There is no one like him, or me, in the world. I am the only one who can produce my thoughts, my ideas, and all of them need to be heard and acknowledged, whether by me, or others around me.

I committed to say to myself: "Today, I commit to be true to myself."

For me, this relationship with my horse was deeper than I had ever had with another human, even Tom. I had been learning that a horse truly knows what is in your heart. It wasn't restricted to just one horse, all horses can read humans, just as the horses in the herd can read each other. They can tell when their human gets scared, and at these times, they take control over their person, or they can connect to the soul of the human and work in harmony. Horses can tell that they are loved, even without being hugged at every opportunity or given treats. They know when your love comes from the heart. They feel good when they are liked and don't feel so good when we are angry - just like humans.

From this I realised the people in my life had talked to me, but not connected with me. Years ago, in a sales training session we learnt about body language and how to get the other person to buy. Communication comes in many forms and sometimes it is not through words. This knowledge about body language and non-verbal communication skills had helped me build upon relationships, influence and provide leadership. Yet, I was now learning about energy shifts, and how these shifts change my whole perspective. This horse was amazing. Taking these skills out to the human world, I could see that when used positively the beneficial effect it had on any human to human relationship, as well as human to horse would be incredible.

When Bundy Bear and I first met, there was an incident that allowed me to understand that he was communicating with me. He made it clear that his life had been difficult before I came into his life and that some of his experiences had been very sad. It was evident to me that his memories were real and had a profound impact on him. I soon learned that Bundy had a deep-seated negative association with men and whips, which had been triggered by Tom's mere presence with the whip. Even though I held the whip and he was frightened, Bundy stayed with me and allowed me to continue. But as soon as

Tom took the whip, Bundy was terrified, and his past memories came flooding back. It was a powerful moment that showed me how deeply ingrained his memories were and how much they still affected him.

That terror was so deep it spoke volumes to both Tom and me. These moments showed up from time to time, with different things that I did with him. Often his reaction was so strong it made me cry, and at other times it made me angry. What had happened to this horse? What had caused the judgement that others had made of his "bad" behaviour? And more to the point, what had they done to him as a way of correction and reprimand?

His progress was slow and often erratic. At times, he would get a flash of the past and then he would lose his mind. As I saw his story unwind I began to lose faith in humanity and the people who called themselves 'professional riders'.

I'd been reading a book written by Dr Andrew McLean about retraining horses and he said the process of retraining a horse often took three times as long as starting with a fresh horse. So, having read that, I knew this horse was going to be a huge journey. He wasn't a blank slate, and his past behaviours kept coming back, so needed to be retrained. Even when I thought I'd got a message across, it would come up again and again in different ways.

It was clear to me that Bundy's reaction and association with men and whips needed to be addressed to prevent any future harm to himself or others. He was a highly sensitive being, and I respected the boundaries he had set for himself. With this in mind, I made a conscious effort to improve our situation. I knew it wouldn't be an easy journey, but I was determined to help Bundy feel safe and secure. My intention was to create a positive environment where he could flourish, and I was willing to do whatever it took to make that happen.

As I led Bundy Bear into the yard, I knew we had some work to do on our connection. This time, I decided to leave his halter off and let him roam free. I walked both of us into the centre of the yard and gently asked him to move away from me while holding the whip in my left hand. At first, he took off at lightning speed, racing around the yard in a wild circle. As I stood there, quietly holding the whip, I couldn't help but notice that he seemed afraid of being pushed away again.

But I wasn't deterred. Since the day of the float training, I had spent countless hours gently rubbing the whip over his body, helping him to see that it wasn't a beating stick but rather a tool to aid in our work together. I knew that building trust with Bundy was a slow process, but I was willing to put in the time and effort to help him feel safe and secure.

He continued to circle the yard, but I stayed calm and focused, allowing him to move at his own pace. Slowly but surely, I could see him beginning to relax and let his guard down. With each gentle stroke of the whip over his body, he became more and more at ease, until finally, he stopped racing around and stood still beside me.

It was a small victory, but it meant everything to me. I knew that our work was far from over, but I also knew that every small step we took together was a step in the right direction.

As he galloped around the arena, I couldn't help but feel a lack of connection between us, as if we were two beings from different worlds. It seemed as though he was simply going through the motions, a beautiful creature expressing the turmoil in his heart. But even as I struggled to understand him, I couldn't help but sense his emotions coursing through me, like a wave of energy that touched me at my core. It was as if his fear and uncertainty had become a part of me, and I was there with him, every step of the way.

I breathed a deep sigh and dropped the whip to see if I got a different response. My aim was to work with only my body, my energy field, breathing and a deep focus. I wanted to remove the emotions that had risen to the surface when I saw his pain. I wanted to be present, and not allow any of my thoughts or emotions to project onto my horse. Basically, I had to stop thinking to get the connection. It was hard work, and took much of my focus, because the more I did it, the more I thought, and caused a disconnection! Yet when it came, I found the process much softer and easier to maintain. The thoughts rolled away, and I was able to just be. With a softness in my body, and soul I asked him to slow down in my head. I visualised him walking and being soft and malleable.

After a while of doing this, I noticed some moments where he began to slow a little and he would turn his inner ear towards me, showing he was listening. I continued for a bit longer, and watched him calm down. Then suddenly he switched off from me and flew to the gate of the yards. He stood there, stock still, yet looking actively around him, ready for a possible escape, if needed. It was as if he had panicked about what he was doing. As if the act of slowing down was something to be scared of.

When he first ignored my request, a storm of emotions swept through me. Frustration washed over me like a wave, knowing how far we had come together. Anger quickly followed, as I couldn't understand why he wasn't listening to me. And with each passing moment, worry began to creep in - was I doing something wrong?

But despite my doubts and fears, I knew that I had to assert my dominance and take control of the situation. I asked him to move away from the gate, determined to make the decision for him to stop, not the other way around. It was a lesson someone had taught me long ago - to never let the horse dictate the terms of our relationship.

I stood a few meters away from him and gently picked up the whip and directed it towards his body. It was a small request, but one that he seemed reluctant to follow. He continued to stand at the gate, gazing out into the world beyond.

And yet, even in that moment of defiance, I couldn't help but feel a sense of connection with him. It was as if we were both working through something together, learning and growing along the way. And as I looked into his eyes, I knew that we were in this together - two souls on a journey towards understanding and trust.

Despite seeing small changes in his responses and feeling like he was starting to trust me, I couldn't shake off the feeling of uncertainty. As I stood there in the middle of the yard, I wondered what my next move should be. Was I doing the right thing? Was I building a connection with him or pushing him too far away?

I looked back on my past experiences with horses and all the literature I had read on the subject. But even with all that knowledge, I still wasn't sure. It was like walking a tightrope - one misstep and everything could come crashing down. But at the same time, I knew that I had to take that leap of faith, to trust myself and my instincts, and to trust him.

And as I watched him from across the yard, I knew that our journey together would be full of twists and turns. But I also knew that, no matter what, I would always be there for him - to guide him, to teach him, and to learn from him. For in that moment, we were not just horse and human, but two souls on a path towards connection, trust, and understanding.

Maybe I should let him stand at the gate, where he was comfortable and felt safer. Maybe when he did that, the right thing would be to walk up to him. Yet, I felt that wasn't the answer. One of my beliefs was I needed the horse to react to me, and not for him to take over. This belief was based on my safety. So I dropped the whip and stood still and waited, and watched, allowing the air to move across my face, and watching the mane on his neck flow in the cold breeze. I was well rugged up in the cold, and there was no need to hurry. I wanted to stay where I was and just let him feel my presence, so he knew I was there, yet not threatening him. I would move away only when he felt ready to reconnect with me. I was looking for something, anything that would give me a clue; an eye or ear movement, or a head tilt towards me.

After several long minutes I noticed there was a change. I wanted to jump for joy, I truly was so excited. Yet that was definitely NOT the thing to do in the middle of the yard with a broken horse in there with you. Instead, I allowed my heart to race for a brief moment and then took a deep breath, smiled and continued. I was actually getting this. Through my patience I was building a connection. I knew he was tuning in, because there was a change to his expression and his ear was pointing towards me, even though he continued to face away. In that moment, I knew I had gotten through to him, and that was the connection I was looking for. Softly and slowly we continued the dance, of moving around the yard with Bundy stopping at the gate for respite, yet over time he didn't linger there for long. When asked, instead of bolting off, he would walk on slowly. I wanted to give him the choice, to allow him to decide whether to join in with the game I was trying to play or not. As I asked him to move, it became clear to me that he had made his choice and he wanted to be part of the fun, the dance. At one point, he turned to walk towards me and allowed me to pat him. I asked him into the centre, gave him a scratch along his neck, and he gave a big sigh.

At the end of the session, Bundy Bear followed me around the yard. He was curious, calm and content. This was the start of a totally new communication style with him. During this process I had found a simple way to find a peaceful connection that was filled with trust and confidence. By changing the negative feelings that I held within myself, and ultimately sharing them with my horse, I had changed the way we connected. As I closed the gate after letting him back into his paddock, I felt a huge emotion inside me. I wasn't sure who released it, me or Bundy Bear, yet I knew that it was a huge turning point in our relationship.

It took me several weeks to fully appreciate the impact of that day in the yard with my horse. Looking back, I realised that I had been more than just a leader - I had been a supportive, kind, and curious guide. Instead of bullying my horse into compliance like he had experienced in the past, I had asked questions, listened to his responses, and given him the time and space to make choices.

In doing so, I had removed any judgement or personal feelings from the situation and truly focused on understanding what was taking place. And when I realised the power of this approach, it transformed not just my communication with my horse, but also my interactions at home and at work.

I began to wonder - if horses could communicate with such subtlety and nuance, could the same approach be applied to human relationships? And so, I started to implement these same communication skills with my team. The results were astounding.

By approaching each interaction with openness, curiosity, and kindness, I found that I was able to build stronger connections, foster deeper trust, and ultimately achieve more meaningful results. And as I watched my team grow and thrive under this new approach, I couldn't help but feel a deep sense of gratitude for my horse - for teaching me not just about leadership, but about the beauty and power of authentic communication.

When I got home from work one day, I sat down on the deck and looked across the paddock and the horses. Tom handed me a beer and came and sat with me, placing a bowl of nuts on the table between us.

'Want some company?' he asked.

"I'd love some," I replied smiling.

"How was your day?"

"I've been applying this new thinking and way of being with my team for at least four months now, the way of changing my communication – just as I have with my horses. Looking back I realised I must have seemed very bossy when I told the team what to do and I had been very forthright. But now I see this different way of leading, and it seems to be having a total shift in my staff. It has changed the way they communicate, their connect to each other, and ultimately the results we are getting." I said.

Tom just smiled and took a sip of his beer.

"Now, I am being more curious, asking questions, listening for what and how they respond, and allowing them to make choices, just like I have been doing in the yard with Bundy Bear. From this change I've noticed that in just a few months, the team appeared to be more innovative, forthcoming with ideas generation, and more connected." I went on.

More smiling from Tom. Was that smugness I saw on his face? I took a sip of my beer and looked out at the horses as they walked towards the yards coming in for dinner.

"Almost time to feed the horses," I said pointing towards the yards.

"No, you've still got this beer to finish" Tom said handing me another bottle.

"How did that one go so quickly?" I asked him.

"Must have been thirsty. It's all that reflection you're doing nowadays – thirsty work!" he laughed.

I nodded and continued along my thought path. "Sometimes it is hard to get out of old habits, but I am really making an effort to take steps in the right direction, and I'm super pleased with the results. It really is making my days so much easier. I know I don't always get it right, but now I can realise that, and consider how to do it better next time. The reflection part is easy for me, now I know what I'm looking for"

As I spoke, I realised that that spotty horse was transforming my life for the better. "You know Bundy Bear has an amazing ability to share with me new ways to be my best self. It is almost like he knows exactly what is happening in my life, and he shares an experience for me to work out that helps with my situation. An experience that I need to solve with him, so that I could apply into other areas of my life."

"I think you are right, he certainly is making a change to both of our lives, for the better," Tom said.

"Is he actually communicating with me?

Does he know what I need to know right then and there?

It certainly looks that way." I said putting down my beer and reaching for the nut bowl.

"I'm certainly learning that this horse can tell when I am dedicated to making him listen, and he can also feel when I am going to persevere until he does what I am asking of him. He also can tell if I am likely to give up and just let him misbehave or be alone. He really knows stuff! Stuff that sometimes I don't!"

"What do you mean?" Tom asked.

"I get the feeling that he has an insight into me, my real self. He can tell when I am not being congruent, when my innermost thoughts don't match what I am displaying on the outside... and when it does. Maybe it's in my face, or my body stance, I'm not sure, but he knows!" I replied.

"Huh! That is super cool. By working on your relationship with your horse you ultimately are working on your relationship with yourself, and everyone else in your life. Cool horse. I always knew he was special, even if he pushes through my fences." said Tom.

"Oh goodness, has he broken another fence?" I quickly asked

"No, all good. He was just pushing himself through the one up the back. I saw him the other day. But it is still standing." Tom smiled, reassuring me.

"Thanks, and yes, he is an amazingly cool horse." I said smiling back at him. When did he become that insightful? I pondered. "And I know I am infinitely better for his interactions and his wisdom."ness to me" I continued.

"So am I," Tom said into his beer quiet enough to almost not be heard. Then louder, "Think Bundy, Be Bundy."

Over the next few months I continued to build on the communication with Bundy. I continued working from the ground so that I gained a connection of trust. From there I was able to get in the saddle where he would already be tuned in to my energy and the channel of communication would be open and he could be ridden.

Bundy and I were beginning to enjoy the friendship. Even though there was still so far to go, and much more to learn from and about each other, we were beginning to have fun.

There was a time when I didn't fully grasp the power of my horse's body language. I was so caught up in my own thoughts and expectations, pushing my weight around and assuming others would simply follow suit.

But then, something changed.

I was in the stable preparing for the evening, and I was lost in thought about entering Bundy Bear into an event, one that meant he had to perform in front of others. As I filled buckets and hay nets, I was picturing us galloping across the course and feeling the thrill of the ride. And then, I looked up and saw him. Bundy was looking right at me, and I noticed the tiniest movement in his head - almost like a nod.

At first, I couldn't believe it. Did he really just communicate with me like that? And then, he did it again. That subtle gesture spoke volumes, and suddenly, I realised that my horse had been trying to communicate with me all along.

It was a powerful moment of connection, and it marked the beginning of a new level of understanding between us. From that day forward, I made a conscious effort to truly see and hear my horse, to pay attention to his every movement and gesture. And as I did, I felt our bond grow stronger and deeper than ever before.

I looked around, was there a camera on me... was someone making fun of me? Nope. It was just me and my horse. Oh my, my horse can really talk. I can't hear his words, yet I can see he is really communicating. He stood there looking at me with his deep brown eyes. Then came the doubt, the words of disbelief, the overwhelming rush of thoughts, I didn't see it, I made it up, maybe he was getting a fly off his head. Bundy walked away from me and turned his back. Bundy was done with communicating. I wasn't convinced, but I was curious.

A couple of days later I got talking to my friend Hayley about it. As I told her about it I felt self-conscious, almost like I had imagined it. "Bundy nodded his head to me the other day. Like I asked a question, and he said YES!"

Hayley wasn't surprised at what I said; in fact, she totally concurred and said, "It's no surprise as horses whisper with their body language. The other horses notice a small head nod, or a tiny twitch of the tail, or the intention to pick up a foot with a shift of balance. It is us humans who don't see it."

"Of course!" I said hitting my forehead with the bottom of my palm. "Sometimes it takes me a while to get it."

"You are not alone there, Amanda," Hayley said smiling back at me.

I rolled my eyes in response, smiling inwardly.

"Horses do not want to waste energy in the herd, and to maintain everyone's safety they stay quiet so they don't call the attention of predators with loud noises or hoofbeat vibrations through the ground. So they act in very small ways," said Hayley.

"And that is exactly what I had seen that day." I said "I think he's learning to talk human!"

After that conversation I started to watch the horses in the paddock. I started to pick up all of these movements. It was then that I knew Bundy Bear was truly communicating with me. I booked him into the event I was thinking about back in the stable, the one where he said YES. We went and had a wonderful time together, in fact it was one of the first times we had actually enjoyed ourselves when we were out.

For me, I knew I had to remain consciously aware of the way I communicated, to my team, to my family, and to my horse. By doing this, and consciously taking a step back to reflect, I would become more conscious and aware of what I had been doing that had caused angst, and how I could make changes to stop it from happening again. I found it interesting that I needed to actually say the words out loud to someone else before I would believe them myself.

LOVE AND EGO

The ego, with its subtle influence, often obstructs our path, and yet we remain unaware of its presence.

"What is love?" I thought to myself one day as I crossed the yard. That weekend when I called my mother, I'd been having a conversation about loving all things, including unconditional love, and it got me wondering.

"What is unconditional love? Is it like what a dog gives to its owner? Love without strings attached. The love that is offered freely without needing anything more (except maybe food, water and a bed in return). And how is that different from ego?" I asked her. Mum had been talking to me about this for years and I knew she would come up with something that I could learn from.

My mother explained to me that unconditional love means loving someone without expecting anything in return. She gave the example of a dog, which loves its owner regardless of how they behave, but still needs food and water. Loving yourself means putting yourself first without being selfish, and taking time to rest and heal when you need it. Ego refers to the idea we have about ourselves and the feelings we have about our own importance.

We didn't continue any further along this line of conversation as I needed to process what she had said. So I asked her about her sister, and how she was getting along following her recent fall. The call went on for some time, but focused back on Mum and her issues.

After that call, I started thinking about our relationships with others. It occurred to me that if we have good relationships with partners and friends who love us unconditionally, they should always be there for us, regardless of conflicts, mistakes, or differing views and goals. In these cases, love is offered for the sake of supporting one another. However, I also realised that as we grow older, our ego can get in the way. As humans, we all have quirks, flaws, and challenges, and not all of our so-called 'friends' are there for us when we need them. Some people can handle our flaws, while others can't and may walk away.

I walked out to the yards, to prepare to muck out the stables and yards. As I walked out under a large tree, I noticed a small bird on the ground. I could see that his wings were bound together with a sticky, string like substance. It looked like tree sap, but I couldn't be sure. The little bird couldn't fly with his wings tethered, so I carefully picked him up and started to pull at the sticky substance. To me this was the only way it could be freed. It was harder than I thought, so I carried the bird inside the stables and sat down on an upturned drum with the bird in my lap.

The little bird lay there calmly whilst I cared for his little body the only way I knew how. As I did I felt like I was being guided by love? "Was this unconditional love?" I pondered as I continued to free his wings.

Once I had done what I could, I carried the bird over to the feed room where it was warm and it wouldn't be bothered by the horses when they came in for the night. I placed it in a cardboard box that I left open. I set up a drip feed for him with some water, sprinkled a few bits of crushed chicken seed out for it and put the bird under a light to keep warm.

To be honest I didn't think the bird would survive the night.

When I got to the yard that morning I saw the little bird perched on the side of the box. It seemed he had found enough energy to get himself up on the side of the box, and for whatever reason he hadn't flown away. I walked cautiously towards it and it remained perched on the side of the box. Slowly I picked up the whole box and quietly walked the bird back to where I had found it. I hoped that it was well enough to fly off. And sure enough as I placed the box down it looked around, tweeted and then flew off to be greeted lovingly by its family.

It filled my heart with love and joy to see this little one flying high. I was grateful to have heard his farewell tweet. Maybe he was waiting to say goodbye to me.

"That was unconditional love. Void of ego, doing what was best for another," I told Tom later.

One of the problems that I faced in this journey of self-discovery as I built my relationship with my horse, was my own ego. As Mum and I had been conversing recently I knew that ego was the image I made up in my mind. My ideal of what I wanted, and how I could be satisfied. As humans, we have a deep need to be heard, yet we are not so good at the ability to hear. We listen, but do we really hear? In my life, I had been constantly feeding my ego, validating my self-worth and my own needs, until I had become aware of what I was doing. As a student at school, a leader at work, and in my family, I thought I had all the answers, yet I wasn't really hearing the questions.

I thought that things were either right or wrong, and I never considered it could be something else, as I actually couldn't see a different path clearly. I wasn't asking the questions, or being curious, or hearing, and when I was being told, I wasn't really listening to the answer.

As I entered and competed in events, I observed a disturbing behaviour that seemed to be accepted as the norm by competitors, pony club riders, parents, and trainers. However, upon closer inspection, I realised that it was a form of abuse towards the horses. Sadly, this behaviour is often congratulated and normalised over time, resulting in its continued practice. In some cases, it even escalates with the use of harsh equipment and severe tools, which experts warn against using. Previously, I would have participated in these practices without a second thought, but my newfound awareness has caused me to view them in a different light. It's as if I had been living with a blindfold on, and now I can see others doing the same.

In my journey so far with my amazing horse, I had learned that horses had emotions, that they could communicate, that they had feelings and took on trauma. When we communicated well with the horse there was a trust so strong that cooperation was imminent for our mutual benefit. So why weren't other people seeing this, the people who had been with horses all their lives? The ones who bred them and rode them and showed them?

So often the horses that belonged to these people were disconnected; they seemed like they had shut down. I would see horses at an event and they seemed fried mentally from getting to that point in their life. I would see people pushing their horses beyond their limits, and all for a blue rosette, and maybe a rug to place upon their horse. Was that a win? Or was it an ego boost for the rider?

When I was a young rider, I had experienced instructors who pushed me and my pony to our limits. Later on, as I got back into riding, I encountered trainers who used various gadgets to force the horses to comply and look a certain way. These devices included side reins, draw reins, martingales, and others, which would be fixed to the horse's mouth or head to maintain a specific posture. As a child, I remembered my mother being advised on what gear I needed for my pony, and she would buy it thinking it was necessary. She would visit the tack shop, seeking something to help my horse behave or maintain a certain frame, only to be presented with a wall of leather and metal items to choose from. The world was making a fortune on creating these gadgets.

My instructors adjusted the noseband on my bridle at the beginning of lessons so that it was pulled so tight it left a depression in the horse's nose when the noseband was released. I was told this was needed, yet it was like torture to me and I couldn't understand how they believed they love and care for their horses so much. I had heard it all from so many instructors, you need to use this, or that, to make your horse go right. As the years had gone on and I had come back into riding, I had noted the situation had not gone away; however it had abated a little.

As a very successful teenage rider, was I so blindly driven to get what I wanted that I put the pressure onto the coaches and trainers to deliver me to that point? Did I seek out coaches who got my pony to do what was needed, even if it was from fear? Or was I actually coming from a loving unconditional way of being, which is what I was trying to achieve? I don't think at that young age I had any idea, now that I was considering it. I believe I was caught up in human ego and the need to win.

I knew deep in my heart that I was no saint, that I had used whips in ways that I shouldn't have done. I recalled being coached to whip the pony as it went around the jumps and I'd heard of practices (and maybe even witnessed them) like lifting the rails as the pony jumped the fence. This practice would allegedly hurt the horse's legs, and make it lift its feet up higher next time it jumped.

Whilst I never had that happen to me directly I was deeply sorry for the pony who had stood by me for so many years, and the other things we had done to him.

I knew I couldn't make amends with my pony from my teenage years, as he was no longer around, yet I did have another chance. A chance to help Mr Bear. It was my role to politely explain to my horse that I would train him to understand the situation and not make him do it out of fear. I sought the goal of a happy horse, rather than a ribbon, which in my mind means a well-trained horse. As it turned out, by taking that extra step to make my horse happy, it also meant many blue ribbons and rugs.

My new learnings on ego have shown me that ego makes a person focus only on the aspects of the physical world that matters to them immediately, without consideration for peace, harmony, happiness, or of the impact on others. I had experienced how people felt superior and had to be constantly right, and how those actions had left people in their wake feeling low and unworthy. I wanted to be authentic and have confidence, and that to me meant considering others and the impact that my actions had on them. Being authentic meant not coming from a place of ego.

During this time I learned there was an important distinction between offering love and forgiveness and continuing to accept the abuse of harmful actions. For me this lesson applied to my human relationships as well as human-horse relationships. Being unconditional with my love meant that I simply accepted them for who they are. I expect the same from others, yet sometimes I learnt the truth of their own insecurities.

My horse has taught me the value of strength in the face of adversity. Through our journey together, I have learned that resilience can grow from difficult situations. He has shown me time and time again that even in the midst of challenging circumstances, there is always a silver lining. One of the most beautiful things I have learned from him is how to embrace challenges and offer love, connection, and understanding in response. By being open to influence and seeking compromise, we can move forward in a way that benefits both of us. This realisation has been a breakthrough for me, allowing me to see the truth of what life is really about. The feelings I have experienced through this journey surpass all others, and I am grateful for the lessons my horse has taught me.

This new strength allowed me to grow in other ways. One of those areas I needed to grow was about learning to set boundaries. So, just as I knew humans are all different, I also knew each horse was, too. I wanted to set comfortable boundaries around the things I didn't want my horse to do. Things that might impact my health, or harm me in some way. Having decided that, I also did not want to entertain any riding instructor who demanded more from him than he was capable of giving at that particular time. I had to choose my instructors carefully.

I wanted to respect Bundy's limits and consider any requests made by the instructor and Bundy's reactions. This meant treating him with love and respect, even while maintaining my boundaries and looking after myself. Sometimes it was hard, as you could be put into a shared lesson with an instructor you hadn't had before. So I would have to set strong and meaningful boundaries.

One day, at the riding club I was placed with an instructor and I was the only one in the lesson. There were others who had booked in, but hadn't turned up. I soon learned that the instructor was one who wouldn't listen to me, or my horse. She had her plan and we needed to fit it. Even when I greeted her and said my horse was in rehabilitation mode, and so he didn't need to be worked hard, she made us work hard. She didn't relent. I complied at first, and then, after Bundy stopped suddenly and wouldn't move, I realised what was going on. I had not set any boundaries with the instructor, and so I was potentially damaging my horse. I stopped and we stood still. She yelled at me to get going. When she had finished her barrage of words, I told her (not really that politely) that I had finished the lesson, and thanked her for her time. For years, I had been told to respect your elders, and that meant coaches, instructors and teachers. I had obeyed what they said and allowed them to convince me their way was best. I would politely do as they said, even though I didn't feel right about it. This time though, I had stood my ground. It was hard for me to stand up to her; but it certainly was necessary, yet it felt wrong.

Boundaries were just the beginning of my realisation of how I was living. Another area where I drew insight was in the way I spoke. I learned through Bundy that I was constantly on 'loud.' Just as horses can turn the volume of their conversation up and down as the need arises, I realised I also needed to become an expert at this.

When I first met Bundy Bear, everything I did was loud or strong. I would walk into the yard with determination and intensity, or ask for something with a forceful tone, like I was demanding it. Once I realised Bundy needed volume control, I had to practise adjusting my inner energy, my tone and volume, for the sake of a mutual conversation. I learnt to understand his response and mimic his language, adjusting my volume with the appropriate intensity. He told me regularly how intense I was, even before I knew it.

Through working with Bundy Bear, I was learning that to be able to listen to myself and my team, I needed to be able to understand what was being said in order to move me forward in life. I practised my volume control with my team, and family. It worked a treat, and this new communication model engaged my team, and ultimately created bonds of trust between us all. I was creating a deep-seated love for my team; and they in turn were beginning to really put in the effort so the team would gain. It wasn't about making myself look good, rather I was getting to know others on a much deeper level. Moving away from my ego driven motives, and more into gaining wisdom. They respected me for this.

BUNDY KEEPS TEACHING

Learning is a precious treasure that accompanies us everywhere, for life never ceases to be our greatest teacher.

There were moments when it seemed that Bundy Bear was forever the teacher and I was just going along for the ride. He was always living in the moment, the here and now. He didn't let the distractions of the past, or the future bother him. He knew what was going on in my world, and he would set about finding ways for me to see another pathway. For instance, he seemed aware of when I didn't have enough time. When I would come home late from work, and think, "I'll quickly work with him," he would use his knowledge to his advantage, and deliberately avoid doing what I wanted him to do. And that would make the task twice as long.

In the beginning, I would charge into the yard with all my energy, ready to tackle whatever task was at hand. But when those tasks took longer than expected and I found myself stuck in the stable for hours on end, I couldn't help but feel angry and frustrated. I would stomp back into the house, creating unnecessary drama.

However, things changed when I met Mr. Bear. He taught me to see those moments of extended time in the yard as a blessing, rather than a curse. They were an opportunity to de-stress from the hectic work environment and truly focus on the present moment. With each passing day, I learned to appreciate these moments and the peace they brought me. No longer did I rush through my work. Instead, I learnt to savour each moment, finding joy in the little things and being able to focus with much more clarity.

My friend, Judy, was someone I had originally met at my riding club. We became good buddies and regularly got together to mostly discuss horses. She was originally from the United Kingdom and in her younger years back in the UK she was an amazing event rider. Today, as I sat across from her having coffee, I noted her sagging shoulders and the general droop that sometimes comes with ageing. She told me, "my body is slowly giving up, so I just plod around on a horse." Yet, when I have seen her on a horse I can see from the way she rides that she was once a beautiful rider.

Over the time I've known her, she has come out to our farm a few times, and we have gone out in the bush together. Judy on Bundy Bear, and me on one of my other ponies. I had seen in these times just what a beautiful, soft and gentle rider Judy was. There are photos on the walls at Judy's house in the WA hills that show her riding in the UK on her horse, Maximilian, over a cross country jump at the world's greatest 5-star equestrian event, the Burghley Horse Trials. To ride in this event is acknowledged globally by leading riders as the ultimate competitive goal.

When I was in my early twenties, I had visited that event and the Badminton Horse Trials. They are two of only five annual four-star competitions worldwide, so it was amazing for me to be able to attend both watching those amazing riders. For me, it was four days of superb competition and watching amazing partnerships. I was awed by the size and complexity of the fences, the distances covered, the people, the stalls, the noise, the money, the trucks and set up of each rider/horse combination, the whole exciting spectacle. It was so inspiring. Thankfully, at both events, falls were pretty few and far between, and whilst I witnessed a couple, they were only minor tumbles in which horses hit fences and then deposited their riders at the bottom of the jump. Both times, the riders got up and walked home without their horse and without any injury. The walk of shame, as it was known.

One of the photos on the wall of Judy's house was of her jumping the Leaf Pit at Burghley – an iconic two-metre drop, which is a leap of faith for the rider, trusting the horse and its capability implicitly. Judy told me when I'd asked, that she'd been told to stop riding altogether by her doctor prior to that photo. Some years earlier, she'd had a tumour removed from her spine and had been told she might never ride again; yet she continued to do so, disregarding the advise. After the tumour was removed she was able to carry on eventing at the top level, and put in many months of effort. However, the demands of her high level of riding eventually caught up with her. A few months before the photo was taken, she received news from her neurologist that she would have to stop riding.

She told me, "I had spent years working up to this and I refused to give up. So I continued my dream as planned. Before long though I had to step away from the big events, and it was then that my engineer husband suggested we move to Australia. It seemed an obvious choice."

I admired her courage, her stamina, and horse sense. She was a very caring rider, and respectful of the horse. I know Maximilian would have been very well looked after during his time carrying her over those huge fences. She became a dressage judge in Australia, and was again highly regarded on the horse scene, although for a different reason now. Judy was someone to admire, and when we became friends we would have regular coffees and enjoy talking about horses for hours, especially Bundy Bear. It was always interesting to learn about her values, and about being a dressage judge.

As much as she loved riding, it was no secret that this kind of activity over a long time and with her condition could take a toll on her body. She had been pushing herself to the limit for years, striving to reach the top of her game. Yet, despite her passion and dedication, it seemed that her body had finally reached its breaking point.

It was just a few short months after that photo was taken she received the news from her neurologist that would change everything. It was devastating for her to learn that she would have to give up riding. She couldn't help but feel like a part of her had been taken away.

But as she looked back on that moment now, she realised that it was just the beginning of a new chapter in her life. Although it was hard to let go of something that had been such a huge part of her identity, she was grateful for the lessons she had learned along the way. And even though she could no longer ride, she knew that she would carry those lessons with her for the rest of her days.

During one of our coffee meetups, we ended up discussing the dressage judges and how they seemed to be projecting their opinions onto the competitors rather than just stating the facts. It was a frustrating realisation, but we understood that the judges' comments on the score sheet were meant to be helpful for riders to improve their skills at home.

The judges provide a score based on what they observed during the test and then give feedback on areas that need improvement and what the rider did well. The only issue was that there was limited space on the sheet, so the notes were often brief and to the point.

Despite the brevity of the comments, we realised that they were invaluable in helping riders to improve their skills and overall performance. It was just a matter of taking the feedback constructively and working on the areas that needed improvement.

Yet, recently it seemed to me that it was a trend for competitors to be told something about their horse that was just an opinion, rather than a fact or something that could help them improve their riding. Judges in dressage are people, and they all come with their own biases; so naturally, even though they may try hard not to be, they are biased towards known riders and the breeding of horses. It frustrated me no end, because I felt I was always up against such comments whilst riding a black and white horse, which was not a "traditional' colour, and I felt that was often against me. Luckily, I had not encountered a comment such as "Nice plaits" or "I am sure a good test is just around the corner!" as I had heard other riders say they had received on their test paper. When the judges turned their attention to aesthetics you knew they were really scraping the bottom of the barrel for positive feedback. I received some comments about my horse riding skills, but they weren't helpful in improving my riding. Instead, they were just people's opinions or things to write, like saying, "lovely mare" when my horse is actually a gelding or saying "has potential," which really meant nothing.

When I received feedback on my horse riding, it wasn't always helpful. Even the judge's comments were confusing and difficult to understand. One common comment I received was "Needs more suppleness." But what exactly did that mean? I couldn't figure out if it meant my horse was moving in a straight line instead of bending around a circle, or if I needed to be more fluid and precise in my movements. Maybe it meant my horse wasn't ready for the specific task, or that he needed to be more responsive to my leg cues. I was left wondering and feeling frustrated.

We had some wonderful laughs over these comments, but often as Judy had not actually seen the test she couldn't provide me with the valuable advice I needed. She did share with me much of her wisdom though and it was always a fun time together.

Anyway, on this particular day, we got talking about egos, and how they affect people and their judgement. Were these judges putting a competitor down in order to feel more important themselves? Or were there physical, emotional, and social needs that were actually the reason behind the decisions? They would never know, but for me, it was an interesting reflection exercise.

When I spoke with Judy, I opened up about my past experiences with making decisions based on my ego. I admitted to her that I used to do things just to ease my anxiety about fitting in, being accepted, or gaining recognition. Looking back, I realised that these choices were driven by my need to compensate for my low self-esteem. I didn't know any better at the time and was simply trying to protect myself.

Years ago, when I was in my final year of school, I had to make some tough choices about my future. I was naturally smart, but I didn't apply myself, so my grades had slipped. At the time, the school directive was to get a good end-of-year score that would allow me to get into certain university courses. But since I didn't know what I wanted to do, I didn't care about my score.

I was very good at science and had come in the top 10% of the State in Human Biology, and the top 20% in Biology. Even so, I didn't aspire to be a doctor, or study anything related to human biology. I also didn't have the Maths or English scores that were required to get into those courses. My mother suggested I become a nurse, which didn't interest me much, but it seemed to be a good idea – as any idea was better than nothing.

Then even this idea didn't inspire me enough to work hard on my scores, and the end result was my overall score was not high enough for me to do Registered Nursing. I could only get into Enrolled Nursing, where I would be awarded a Diploma in Nursing, rather than a University degree. In my eyes, this was unacceptable. My ego took over. I was not someone who just did a Diploma. There was no way I was going to tell my friends I failed to get into Nursing and could only become an Enrolled Nurse. So I never went down that path.

Talking to Judy about that day I laughed and said "I don't think I would've lasted anyway, as I don't really like talking to lots of people!" Maybe the universe was helping me in that decision. I laughed at how my ego had taken over, and about having the feelings in my body as I spoke, even so many years later.

"Hindsight is such a wonderful thing," Judy said. "At the time you did what was right for you and what you knew. You can't undo the past, and now you only have the future, and your decision today is how you wish to move into that future."

Such wise words, I thought.

EMOTIONAL INTELLIGENCE

Stop your negative self-talk – you are always listening.

When I first got Mr. Bear, I thought he would never want to jump again. I had seen his responses from the whip and I associated that with jumping. So for the first three years together, we did fun things that didn't involve jumping.

I loved riding Bundy out in the bush that surrounds the back of the property. He loved it too; I felt him get excited as we left the gate, and he would trot or canter in places where he felt safe. For me, it was a healing space. The "bush" at the back of our place was full of hills, valleys and cleared tracks for ease of firefighting equipment to get in if needed. This made riding in the bush easy. It was a forest of trees, of red gums, jarrah and open woodlands of marri, wandoo and flooded gum, and the understory had some of the most brilliant wildflowers and native shrubs. We would often see wildlife along the way, such as kangaroos, wallabies and emus. The Darling Scarp where we lived hosted a huge variety of indigenous species of flora and fauna and was recognised as some of the most diverse in the world. This made the area botanically rich and historically unique. Sadly, it was also used as a place for locals to dump their rubbish, so when we rode out we would often see tyre tracks and then a pile of household rubbish.

The ground was sandy in patches and gravel in others. The bush was peaceful, even though it was filled with native animals and creatures that would often jump across your path, scaring both rider and horse at times!

I would look at the wildlife as I passed, a bush or tree, or flower or even a kangaroo or deer or emu, looking at everything with wonderment. This process became a way of looking that opened a window onto an inner field within one that held emotion. A field that was operating in my life in the background all the time, yet a place I was not aware of. By focusing on these features, I was experiencing something like opening up. Every time I looked at something it would impart its unique emotional sense. This sense could only be noticed when just looking at the thing, and cannot be noticed while I was trying to figure out what it actually was. It was like a shift in my brain, moving from my prefrontal cortex, and thinking about, to somewhere deeper, in my brain and body and feeling it.

So going out into the bush was often a sort of initiation of unique emotions. Each bush or tree was a little door with a surprise inside. What feeling will this one give me? What about that one? These feelings would allow me to connect dots, of issues I was having at work, or projects that seemed to be stuck. They enlightened me to a new way of thinking. Of course I was on Mr Bear, and I also believe he had an input into these feelings in some way.

One day, while riding in the bush, holding the end of the reins, but without any contact with the horse's mouth, Bundy Bear and I were cantering. During the ride, Bundy Bear looked to the left and then suddenly cantered into the bush and jumped over a smallish log. Throughout the entire experience, I held onto the end of the reins but allowed Bundy Bear to move as he pleased. I often rode just with my legs, fantasising that one day I'll ride him out in the bush with nothing on his head. I sat there quietly, as he went into the bush, intrigued as to what he wanted to do. I didn't pull on his reins, instead I allowed him to take me over the log and to feel his response afterwards. He felt alive as if he wanted to do it some more. I came to a stop laughing, and patted him, all the while asking him if he wanted to start jumping again. He seemed keen, so I decided I would test my theory and I looked around to find some other logs to jump. I turned around and felt his excitement as I cantered up to the logs, and over them. As he was very keen to jump them, I seemed to think the answer was yes, he was ready to jump again.

So I enrolled into a jumping lesson the following week. It was run by the Dressage club and the aim was to help dressage horses with their flexibility and confidence. I knew dressage horses don't usually jump, so the height of the fences would be low.

It sounded perfect, especially as it was over two days.

I turned up to the event excited to be able to actually jump again. I got there early and watched the other riders as they went through their paces. Bundy Bear, it seemed, was not so excited. He took one look at the arena, at the jumps in it, regardless that they were small, and he started getting extremely nervous. I decided to walk him around, and try to calm him before his lesson time. I walked him away from the arena, where I could still see what was happening, but not hear the instructor. He seemed calm enough when he was that distance, so I sat cross legged on the grass and allowed him to eat, hoping by the time our lesson came he would've settled.

At the designated time, I saddled him up and walked into the arena. Thankfully there was only another horse and rider in my class. We walked and halted in the middle of the arena to introduce ourselves. Bundy Bear stood initially as the instructor greeted us and got to know a bit about our horses. I explained whilst he had jumped in the past, he hadn't jumped for a while and this was his first time in two years.

She asked the horses to start walking around the arena past the jumps. Immediately Bundy Bear reacted. He reared up, turned and wanted to flee out of the space. My initial reaction was to take control, but I knew that had a chance of increasing his fear levels. So I tried to keep him calm, and noticed he had started to sweat profusely.

I could feel panic arising in his body, through his jerky movements and rapid heart rate. He felt like he was a bundle of muscle about to explode. This in turn created a sense of fear in me, and a feeling of being out of control. When he went anywhere near the jump wings, the metal sides that hold up a show jump, he would react by snorting, and jigging on the spot. I knew instantly I needed to calm myself first. I had to have responsibility and control. So I started thinking calming thoughts, and just being. I also realised my aim for this lesson was to just get something small from him. Something like a positive step of calm before I left the arena. My need was to take things slowly and try and get his confidence back.

The instructor was amazing, and had a wealth of experience working with young horses, and so she tried a couple of tactics, taking things really slowly. She put the poles on the ground and asked him to walk over them. When the poles were just on the ground he could do that. But the minute the instructor asked us to walk slowly over them when they were on the ground between the wings, he leapt in the air jumping so high it was surprising I wasn't dislodged from the saddle. As he galloped off from the poles, his tail was tucked between his legs and his head was high. He was totally frightened of these poles between the wings. His reaction told me he was completely disconnected from me and the instructor, and everything else around him. He was focusing only on those poles! In his mind, those poles were the scariest thing in the world.

During a sixty-minute horse riding session, I felt the pressure of making sure the other rider had enough time for their lesson. I wanted to alleviate their stress so they could focus and learn effectively. I wanted to reduce his anxiety, so that he was calm enough to listen and learn. At first, it was difficult to get Bundy, to listen to me amidst all the commotion. However, the instructor was understanding and spoke calmly, providing me with ways to support Bundy.

At one point, when Bundy was behaving better, the instructor asked us to stand to the side while she worked with the other rider. Then she invited us back to try again. Bundy still reacted, but not as severely as before. This process of going over obstacles and then stopping to let Bundy process what was happening was repeated a few times.

Finally, we could see small amounts progress. Bundy was able to walk over the obstacles without galloping off in total panic and causing a scene. The whole process took the entire hour of the lesson, and I was grateful for the other rider and their understanding horse.

I was ecstatic and I wanted Bundy to feel he had done well. . He had definitely become more malleable towards the end of the session.

I knew he would process what had happened, as he stood at the float eating his lunch. I hoped this processing would mean a change in his reactions in the afternoon lesson. The second lesson that day came and I saddled him up. I was keen to see if he would react again, or if he had learnt something from the morning. Sadly he was still scared, but he did make some significant positive steps forward. We managed to not only walk but trot over the poles on the ground without any bucks - just a slightly less terrified gallop afterwards. This to me was a huge sign of improvement. As I watched the other riders that day I found a moment to ask the instructor quietly what she thought had happened to my horse to make him react so violently. She shook her head sadly, and told me she believed he had been subjected to the rapping, or raising of poles on his legs as he jumped. She also wondered if he had been chased by someone from behind a jump. He just reacted like he was looking out for someone to jump out..

During our lesson the next day, my student was still nervous, but I noticed a slight improvement in his reactions. He would still shy away from the wings as we passed them, but he didn't react after we went over them. It was clear to everyone watching that he was terrified of the wings.

Our instructor was very experienced in the world of show jumping at high levels around the world. She explained that she had seen these practices many times before and the resulting damage to horses. She wondered if some people had hidden behind the wings and whipped the poor horse as he jump, with the intention of preventing him from hitting the rails. She suspected that other bad practices had been used on Bundy Bear based but she didn't really get into much detail. I shudder to think what else they might have done.

Cruelty can come from many training practices, she explained, including the way the rider rides, the equipment used on the horse, and relying on force and training mechanisms designed to "force" horses. Things like anger issues from the rider, excessive whipping, harsh pulling or yanking off the bit, and excessive use of the spur.

This was the first time someone outside had actually expressed to me the cruelty that may have happened to Bundy. I was shocked and deeply saddened and vowed to help this poor horse in every way I could.

I was just an amateur rider, and my experience didn't run deep like so many other riders out in the horse rings. So even though I wanted to be a good horse person I found it difficult to always understand what I needed to do, or how he was feeling. In the past two years Bundy had taught me to stop and listen, but this response he was giving now, was up another level. I was dealing with an animal that had his own brain, and I had to read his reactions so that I could guide him in the best way possible. In all of this, I had to accept that when his fear became so high he couldn't help that he was flighty or spooky, and this was a response to being a flight animal.

The whole time I had been riding him, I'd tried to build upon our foundation, so that if and when things went askew, he had some solid support there to help him. We had worked on our communication and up to this point it was going well. Whilst riding dressage we had been communicating about the size of a circle or how steep a sideways movement such as a leg yield is. Whilst I felt we had come a long way, I knew our communication practice was ongoing. It was this foundation that allowed us to build upon his jumping work, and create change.

Over the next few months we progressed from poles to jumps, and whilst he would now go over fences with wings on, he was still jittery and scared of many things in a jump arena. While jumping though our communication seemed to have gone out the window. Bundy felt the need to be in control in order to avoid pain and successfully jump the fence. However, when it was his responsibility to put in the strides to clear the fence, he would often gallop at it and then crash through it. I recognised that this behaviour was rooted in fear. Ideally, he should have been able to trust his own abilities and make decisions for himself, but his past experiences made him unable to do so. As a result, when he was in control, he would either gallop off, suddenly stop, or crash through fences.

Riding him when he was in this kind of mental state was not enjoyable, as I often found myself face-planting his mane or being dislodged from the saddle and having to cling back on before approaching the next fence. He would also try to buck me off if my dislodged leg accidentally kicked him in the flanks. It was a huge risk, but I was determined to help him, so I remained calm and did my best.

I knew that he had the ability to jump, as I had seen him clear fences over 120cm high in competition before he came into my care. However, to build his confidence, we continued jumping low fences.

What I needed was for him to overcome his emotions, reduce his stress, and be able to jump without fear. My goal was to be so connected that when we did gallop on purpose across the cross country he was with me, and against me. Whilst I recognised the risk to me of training him over jumps, I started to wonder how else I could help him. I continued to do pole work at home, and small cavaletti type jumps to build his muscles back up, and to allow him to trust the whole new situation he was in. If I felt he didn't want to jump I would have stopped, but I really did feel he wanted to keep going. Yet, I hoped I could do more, and wondered if maybe I could help with some training on my mindset too. So I undertook some coaching for myself in emotional intelligence, hoping it would give me some insights into how to help my horse.

According to psychologists, Travis Bradberry and Jean Greaves, co-authors of Emotional Intelligence and Emotional Intelligence 2.0, there are four key areas, or competencies, that make up emotional intelligence: self-awareness, self-management, social awareness, and relationship management. Each involves either personal competence, skills that relate to yourself, or social competence which is skills related to how you interact with others.

The personal competencies include self-awareness and self-management. Self-awareness is a foundational skill for life, and one that I had actually been working hard on with communicating to Bundy. I knew from practice now that self-awareness helped me to understand what I was motivated by, what emotions I was experiencing at a given time, and what "pushed my buttons." This insight had helped me to recognise my own emotional triggers, or causes of an emotional response, and with this information I had a choice of how to react, or stop a negative reaction. It didn't work all the time, but I was still on L plates!

I had started to bring this way of being into everything I did, as a leader at work or with my horse, as a friend, and confidant. These new skills that I was applying in my life were helping me to perceive, use, understand, and manage my emotions in a better way. I was working on being my best self, and I was the person who could make the change. I didn't need to wait for someone else to help me, or do something for me. I could do it myself.

I read that what I was doing was actually a strong part of being emotionally intelligent. Being emotionally intelligent meant that I could tune into my own emotions, as well as the effect they had on others around me, including myself. This also meant I was able to intuitively tune into the emotions of my team and my horse and how these emotions affected me. It was interesting for me to read that this was a "thing."

This practice meant that whilst I was with my horse I could become aware of my emotional triggers, such as his reaction to jumping, which gave me the capacity to try and control my thoughts and reactions. When I was able to, it meant I could make decisions calmly and with confidence; so that my emotions weren't taking control. In essence, I was becoming more peaceful. I needed to trust myself throughout the whole time. Trust that my reactions would be right, and of benefit to him.

The self-management part of the four areas as presented by Travis

Bradberry involves how you react to your emotions. I was learning that people skilled in self-management are flexible enough to direct their emotional responses toward a productive solution. However, emotions can be difficult to navigate and when fear appears it can be completely paralysing. So I needed to get to a point where I could recognise the trigger and change the course of my reaction and channel my behaviour to a positive end. Easy to say, hard to do.

The other two competencies were about social awareness and relationship management. Social awareness is defined as the ability to pick up on emotions in other people and understand their causes. In a way, it means perceiving what others are thinking and feeling, without it being mind-reading. So at work I had to make sure I had conversations about the emotions of the people around me. My tactic here was to stay quiet, ask, and listen carefully without thinking about what you'll say next. Bundy had taught me that skill. Yet, I still needed to be reminded to apply it in my arena.

The relationship management is all about the ability to use awareness of my emotions and the emotions of others to successfully manage relationships. This skill was at its heart all about connection and, once again, the ability to ask and listen effectively. Skills I continually needed with a broken horse.

As an authentic leader, the leader I wanted to be, for my horse and humans, I learnt I needed to share my emotional intelligence by leading from the heart — not from my ego.

MANAGING EMOTIONS

Be mindful of the power our thoughts hold over us. When we confront our worries we find ways to be our own master.

Learning how to understand and manage my emotions appropriately took a long time and lots of effort. Just like implementing any new habit, there were many times when I found myself in hard, stressful, emotionally fraught circumstances. I knew this was part of life, yet my new skills enabled me to tap into a liberating truth. It provided me with the knowledge of somehow being in control and having a choice in how I handled a given situation.

I had to constantly remind myself that effectively managing my emotions did not mean suppressing them. In fact, there were times when it was important to be vulnerable and share my strengths and weaknesses with my team. By doing so, I demonstrated that I had nothing to hide and communicated with them directly and honestly. This approach built trust among my team and encouraged them to feel comfortable sharing their own mistakes. By showing up as an authentic leader and being open about my humanity, I found that people actually appreciated this quality. It didn't cause anyone to lose faith in me, as I had originally feared. On the contrary, it was an attractive quality that brought the team closer together.

Instead of suppressing my emotional responses, I made a conscious effort to tune into them and allow myself to experience them in a healthy manner. I believed that this approach showed my team that I was a real person, with both strengths and weaknesses. At times, I needed to be vulnerable and share my vulnerabilities with my team in order to communicate directly and build trust. I knew that this approach would encourage my team to also share their own mistakes and vulnerabilities, which would ultimately benefit everyone. Over time, I saw that this approach did make a positive change, as my team became more comfortable with sharing their errors and weaknesses.

At work on a Tuesday morning after a long weekend, I saw it come to light. We were all in our early morning meeting huddle, and Tanya, one of my teammates, shared that she had made a mistake last week with something she had placed on the internet. We all considered what she had done, and thought of any implications. As we stood in the huddle, I heard team members rally forth with great suggestions on ways to move forward. To me, it felt like a great wave of support had come over us all. This mistake could've been taken badly, yet it wasn't and it actually turned into a positive event. I saw this as proof that my new way of listening and being aware, with my horse, and my team was certainly to everyone's advantage.

I wanted to be an authentic leader, where people saw that I was human too. I was beginning to see that rather than people losing faith in me, it actually was an attractive quality.

If only I had known about it earlier in life, or even been taught it in school. Learning to communicate with emotional intelligence, and self-awareness was something that would have equipped me to build strong relationships with my teachers and classmates. It would allow me to understand my emotions and I could better manage them rather than letting them control me. This regulation of self would have helped me in stressful situations as well as later in life, with friends and group interactions. Having learnt these skills, I now believed that if I had been taught them earlier in life they would've made a difference to my academic results, and ability to deal with negative emotions that disrupted my learning, and probably my life.

I found whilst working with Bundy Bear that he became my continual barometer telling me how my emotions were going. If I arrived in the yard happy, or mad at him, or angry or stressed from something someone else had done he would clearly show me what was happening and behave in a way that made me stop and think. He was picking up on my emotions and reacting to them. He became the best teaching aid I had. Once I'd realised that my emotions were taking control of me, and my self-awareness allowed me to realise what was happening, I could make a change. So it was becoming very clear to me that he helped me, whilst I was helping him.

This also showed up when I was confident and acted in a certain way, as opposed to being uncertain, nervous or unfocused. It turned out that it didn't matter what it was, my feelings altered my behaviour and Bundy Bear was able to pick that up incredibly well.

I learnt this rapidly when I started to move Bundy Bear into jumping.

Horses communicate in ways that are different from humans. In their world, they use energy and their entire body to communicate, including their ears, tail swishing, lifting a foot, body angle, and even biting. Everything that a horse does, even when standing still, has meaning to other horses.

They also communicate using their voice and can nicker, squeal, or make a louder neigh. The "nicker" sound is a greeting to a human, or to each other. The squeal happens when meeting a new horse to say, "I'm big and scary!" and the whinny or neigh is used to locate lost members of the tribe.

Whilst we humans are blessed with verbal communication, we also use non-verbal ways as horses do. Over time we have reduced our reliance on other cues, and so communicating is often thought of as just what you say. Communicating effectively is about understanding the other person, their emotions, and their intentions. I realised this when I was communicating with Bundy Bear.

The first step I took was to be intentional and clear in everything I did. That way he would be able to take my cues and respond positively. I wanted to connect with him so that he felt listened to, accepted and understood. So my cue had to be clear, and yet not harsh. Something I soon realised applied to humans, having clarity to tell others exactly what I wanted, thought, believed, and felt. Providing clear communication was a way of being honest and allowed me to express myself candidly without being rude or aggressive. Horses are very honest communicators.

To communicate clearly I needed to go back to self-awareness and listening skills. Bundy Bear was also very clear in his response, and I found when I took my time to reflect back on how he perceived the message, the biggest changes would occur. Sometimes, however, his message was hard for me to take, as I thought I was being clear, yet he would say otherwise.

One day, whilst working Bundy from the ground, I had him on a long rope that allowed him to go around me. I had asked for softness, and got his attention. This particular day he was being hugely intuitive, and a sensitive reactive boy. He required me to have a bit of politeness, leadership and just the right amount of sensitivity.

When I asked him to begin to move away, I gave a guiding hand and positive body language towards his flank. He responded and I allowed a few minutes for him to take in his surroundings. I had learnt that Bundy Bear is nosey and he likes to look about before tuning in to me. Once I felt he'd had a good look I brought his focus back to me with my breath and body language.

I wanted to work on his transitions, going from walk to trot and trot to walk before I tried any canter work. I was looking to see if he was confident enough to walk without coming back to a sudden halt, which he had already done a few times. To me, he appeared happy and expressive in his moves between transitions with lovely paces.

I was so excited with how he was showing up that I asked him to canter with a crack of the whip. He leapt into the air and started galloping around. He instantly went from being calm, and soft to being scared, and hard. The feedback from him was instant, and not what I had expected. Just like in life, I had to take it, and quickly make a change to the way I was. I steadied my breathing, as it had by now increased, and asked Bundy to come back to walk. They commenced the same process again, and this time with a softer request to canter. It worked beautifully.

Communicating clearly is also about using the correct medium for the message and ensuring that the other parties understand the message as intended. The medium was important to me and Mr Bear reminded me often. For example, I knew when I kicked my legs too hard whilst riding him but all he needed was a simple energy exchange, he'd tell me by reacting strongly. It came back to me either whispering or shouting. The kick was like a shout, a thought more like a whisper.

Just like the exchange with Bundy in all our communications, less is often more. A light, gentle touch can bring about a significant response from him when sometimes stronger and more forceful handling can create a battleground.

Over the time I'd been riding him, I was beginning to see that communicating clearly to Bundy Bear was all about providing connection and building trust. That meant using my body, energy and breath. This meant riding was easier, and less taxing on my body, as I had learnt that by building that connection, there was no need for forced action just a small request. When speaking to a horse you provide the request. There is no need to add extra words, or an explanation. I also used this tactic with my team at work, making sure I was clear in my communication, I avoided jargon and kept the message simple. This meant everyone understood the message.

Confidence is energy and also forms another area of communication. Our confidence is just like the rest of nature and it ebbs and flows. There are days when my confidence is high, when I feel happy within myself and also comfortable within my surroundings. Other times my surroundings, or vibes from others in the room have an effect on me and my confidence decreases. This means too, there are times when I'm not able to speak up, or say the words I actually want.

Now, this is an area Bundy Bear was always teaching me. If I came into his yard lacking any confidence, he would push right through me, or sometimes walk away. Yet, when I was calm and confident, he would respect me, and standstill, or walk up to me. So even though my confidence would ebb and flow, he was a reminder of just how I was at that moment. Horses communicate through energy, and confidence is a form of energy. The energy of confidence comes out of your pores, and they can pick up on it. So often I saw this in the equine facilitation sessions.

Just as with the horses, if in our closest relationships, we feel pressured, unhappy and under stress, then it becomes very difficult to find a peaceful place. This is where our self-awareness and personal empowerment are very useful. I soon learnt that once I arrived in the space where the horses were, I needed to take a deep sigh and breathe away any of the day's negative energy. This was my peaceful space.

By breathing deeply and opening my heart, I was able to create a new positive feeling within myself. This technique was very effective with my horse, and he provided me with valuable feedback. I found that deep breathing was a powerful tool that could be used in various situations, such as before a meeting at work or at home. It enabled me to leave problems behind and move forward without distractions. By breathing away my worries and negative feelings, I was able to relax and think more clearly. This not only helped me think clearly but also helped me to make positive decisions in my life.

I gradually improved my ability to connect with my true self and aimed to maintain this awareness in my daily life. By doing so, I was able to view stressful situations as a natural part of life and continue on my journey of personal growth and empowerment through self-awareness.

Hayley and I were often on the same wavelength and one day after a ride out together we were sitting on the decking drinking cups of tea, and reflecting on the changes we were making in our lives.

"Imagine you have a 'friend' who seems to question your ideas, and even belittles you," I said. "They stand tall in your space and make you feel rather small and ineffective. Then after a while you begin to notice you change when this person is around, your stress levels rise and uncertainty creeps in. In the past, I would have shrunk away, said nothing and maybe retreated into a corner. When this is unconscious you can't do anything about it, yet when you are aware you can. So once you recognise the situation you have the chance to make some much needed changes. Now I stop and take a huge breath, a pause long enough for me to really feel the change, and the atmosphere changes completely. It truly is amazing."

"Yes, I still do that," said Hayley laughing. It was a small laugh, then as we both sat silently, letting the words sink in, she roared with laughter. A huge belly laugh.

When she was finished I looked at her expectantly.

"Oh, Bundy Bear," she finally said "you are the most incredible boy who has so much to offer us all. Thank you for being you and sharing with me a way of changing my life. I love you to bits."

I sat smiling.

It was these conversations that helped me to see what was happening elsewhere in my life. Even though I could see clearly whilst on the decking and looking across the paddocks, I still had blockages in other areas of my life. Just the other day, as I sat in my office after a colleague had left, I felt a sense of pressure, of neediness, as they left. I stopped and felt into my body and realised just what an impact they were having on me. As he walked out I recognised my pulse racing, and emotions going all over the place. No, it wasn't anything sexual, it was something else. He had this ability to continually question my ideas, and I noticed that I felt belittled. My stress levels had risen and uncertainty was creeping in. I sat and pondered, and allowing myself this time I recalled times when he had stood tall into my space and tried to make me feel small and ineffective. I realised this had been going on for a few months, and unconsciously I hadn't noticed. It wasn't until I became aware that I could do something about it. So now that I recognised the situation I was able to take the chance to make those changes.

TAKING THE JOY AS IT COMES

By finding joy in both big and small experiences, we cultivate gratitude, resilience, and a deeper appreciation for the beauty that surrounds us.

When I acknowledged how I felt I could find joy and friendship with my horse. One morning as I walked into the stable area to feed the horses, Bundy Bear lifted his head and nickered to me. This low-pitched, guttural sound made my heart swell with joy that my horse was welcoming me to the day. His ears would be pricked and a soft nicker of companionable greeting would come every time he saw me. "Hi! Good to see you. Come talk to me!" it seemed he said.

His clarity in his greeting set me up for a beautiful day. It was like receiving a smile from a colleague, or a simple welcome. His nicker was a way of broadcasting how he was feeling, which also brought about health and emotional benefits, including an elevated mood. I smiled at work when doing something that I didn't necessarily like, which in turn helped me to feel much more positive about the task at hand. It was infectious, and people smiled back at me, which made for a happy day.

This feeling of acknowledging a simple smile extended into other areas of my life. It wasn't just the release of serotonin as I smiled, which brought on the natural antidepressant, it was the consciousness of the act. It was quick and easy and had a huge impact. So I kept doing it. When I smiled, other people automatically thought I was more likeable and warmed towards me much quicker, and perceived me as being more confident and sociable.

It impacted my communication and my capacity to feel my energy. When I was with my horse I needed to feel how Bundy Bear was before I could ask and get a good response. So before I did anything I would take time to feel into his mood. Was he happy? Was he sad? Was he worried about what was about to happen? I had to be an active listener. For Bundy Bear, that simple observation and curiosity made him more interested in me because I was showing him I was really interested in him. Which in turn made the riding experience very pleasurable.

Once again I took this skill to my other interactions. Once a month I travelled into the Perth head office to have a management meeting with other senior leaders in it. I didn't know at the time, but I was about to have a clear demonstration of how it could be played out in the corporate sector. On a very wet Monday morning I entered the Board room, coffee in hand and my note paper in the other. I don't like taking my phone into meetings, especially ones where I need to really concentrate.

No one was in the room yet, so I placed my book and coffee cup down and walked over to the window. Our building was high above the Swan River and the board room had a massive window that allowed you to see across the city beyond the river to the Indian Ocean. It was truly magical.

This meeting was important for me to be heard, and when I wanted changes to happen with my team, I needed to speak up. So I took the time to listen to myself first. "Be Bundy" I thought to myself. I tuned in to my mind and recognised what was running through my thoughts. Once I did this, I cleared away the clutter and created a space to make room to hear others.

For me there was a commercial cost to not listening. I wanted my team to be successful, and so I had to be at the top of my game.

As I stood there with my back to the room I heard others entering and sitting down, so I took a couple of deep breaths and walked to the water station and poured myself a glass of water. Taking my water back to my seat, I sat down.

The company I worked for had international offices, and the head office was based out of Melbourne. Our CEO, John Winter, had been to Los Angeles and had come to Perth to see us before heading back to Victoria. He had literally just flown in, travelling straight from the airport to our building for this meeting.

As he walked into the door he placed his suitcase just inside the door, and then his notebook at the place reserved for him. Rather than sitting down, he stayed standing, pulled his phone out of his pocket, and turned it off. I saw him take a deep breath, he focused briefly on the view outside, smiled and sat down. I looked around the room and saw a couple of others also take their phones out and turn them off or to silent. I smiled inwardly.

I knew he had been pre-briefed before entering the room. So I expected he would start the meeting straight away.

"Hello everyone," he began and I prepared myself to be quoted data, facts, and inconsistencies. Instead, he looked around the room and with that same smile he opened the meeting by telling the room that he was interested in everyone and what the world looked like for them.

He then looked across to Jenny, our State Manager, who was sitting next to me and asked, "So what is the biggest challenge you are experiencing, and how can we help you?"

Jenny looked up and said what was challenging her team, our division.

As she spoke he was fully tuned in and completely focused.

He continued to ask her questions. "Tell me more," he would ask or "and what else" or "what do you think about that?"

When he had enough he moved around the room asking questions similar to "What are you struggling with, and how can we help you?"

He didn't solve any problems in the meeting, yet he explored each of them by asking relevant questions, "tell me how that plays out" or "how does that impact our customers?"

When he came to me it was so cathartic to really feel heard. I loved the fact we could look at the issue from the customers view point, and I had some great points to bring forth. I was secretly proud of how I handled myself, and the responses I gave.

It felt the room actually said the words they wanted to say, and I could feel this lightness amongst the group. Everyone had a chance to contribute and everyone had a chance to hear the others.

Before we finished the meeting, John summarised what he'd heard, and then asked, "If I come back in a year, how will I know it's different?"

He looked at Jenny and she said "Well, we will have this system in place, and she went on to describe what would be happening."

"Great," said John, "Then that is your action Jenny, to make sure that system is implemented" he got up, and said "My work is done. I look forward to hearing your updates on progress, Jenny" he took his bag and left the office.

I looked around and felt the best I ever had following one of those meetings. Everyone else was still in their seats, almost stunned.

"I felt really heard," I said to Paul who was sitting on my left.

"So did I," he replied.

We got up and left together. Both of us agreed how brilliant the meeting was, and that we knew that system would be implemented.

Paul said, "I believe it was his genuine curiosity, and his ability to really extract information from everyone, that made us feel heard."

"I agree, he really knew what to ask us, and from that he could find the critical pain point, which we all seemed to have," I said. "It was wonderful to be there in the room, and witness that experience."

"One huge step for mankind," Paul said before we parted to our respective offices.

This experience was very important for me because it helped me to become more curious and ask more questions to better understand the other person and their needs. I learned that when I'm listening to someone, the best thing I can do is to focus entirely on them, not to think about anything else or plan my response while they're speaking. Instead, I listen carefully so that I can repeat what they said to show that I understand. I needed to be like Bundy. This approach helped me to see things from the other person's perspective, build trust, and demonstrate empathy.

In the past, I had thought I needed to respond and act like I knew what I was talking about. This thinking about what I 'knew' prevented me from seeing things as they really are. So often I got stuck in my own thoughts and my mind's unhelpful stories that I actually had nothing worthwhile saying, and blurted out something totally inappropriate instead. This meant that I viewed people, events and the world around me through a veil of preconceived judgements, which hooked myself into negativity, fear and pain.

The process of being less harsh, critical and mean to myself began to ripple out and affect every aspect of my life. It connected and transformed the mind in ways that were truly profound.

JUDY

There are certain moments when someone unexpectedly enters your life, carrying with them a profound lesson meant for you.

Saturday morning I jumped out of bed early to prepare to go and pencil with Judy. She was Judging dressage at a horse trials event and I was nominated as her penciller.

It was only three degrees Celsius outside and I was freezing. I got dressed straight away into many layers, and placed my gloves into my bag. Walking to the kitchen I prepared a quick breakfast of coffee and muesli, checked my bag had everything I needed and then sat down to eat. I prepared instructions for Tom on what to do with the horses. As I grabbed my bag with various layers of clothing, sunglasses, water bottles and lunch, I saw Tom stumbling out of bed. Waving goodbye and blowing him an air kiss, I raced to the car. We were due to be starting at 7am, and would judge horses for the next six hours. Even though I didn't have far to go, I was running a tad late.

Once at the show, I parked my car and walked quickly to where the judging was. I found Judy in the administration tent and I could see she was head down in reflection. She was ready and waiting for me. From previous experience I knew she is often quiet and contemplative before any judging. I was careful not to make idle chatter with her. Collecting my folder of tests, I walked over to her and acknowledged I was ready, holding the red folder up to let her know I had the test. We walked to her car to drive it to the arena for the judging. The tests we were judging required two judges and Judy was the higher level judge; so she parked her car at the short end where the marker was.

I buried my head into the paperwork and prepared my freezing fingers to be ready for the onslaught of words. Judy was typically a good judge to work with. She gave shorter sentences, and didn't ramble. Other judges I had pencilled for could be very verbose. I only had a small space to write notes, and when they would tell a novel to the rider I was expected to write it all down – and fast. Pencilling is a very important job where dressage competitions are held, and are nearly as important as the judge sitting beside you. As a penciller, you are required to record the judges' comments and applicable scores against each movement on paper. Judges depend upon the writer to record their comments and marks quickly, accurately, legibly, and quietly.

The arena was situated in a paddock alongside many other arenas. There was a good view from my place in the car to look at other horses as they came and went. This morning there was fog sitting low, but we could see the end of the arena, which was a bonus. This event was one I had ridden at before, and hoped to be riding at again one day.

The first horse and rider arrived and we started. My hands were sufficiently warmed up, and lucky for me they worked. As the cool air and the fog lifted, horse after horse presented themselves to the judges and rode their test. At some point in the morning we had a break of riders. We both let out a sigh of relief.

"Phew, that was a huge section. Luckily the fog lifted early, I was having trouble seeing the end of the arena," Judy said as she started to get out of the car to stretch herself. I wondered how she gave an accurate score when she couldn't see the other end, but didn't say anything.

"Do you need to go to the ladies?" I enquired.

"No, just stretch. I wish they'd bring some coffee. I'm desperate for one, and a nice slice of cake." Judy replied.

"I'll go find someone and tell them you need some," I said, getting out of the car to find the volunteer who was on morning tea duty. I quickly located someone with a safety vest on, and told them we required refreshments and walked back to the car. Within minutes someone came out and took our order. Luckily the coffee and cakes were delivered to Judy before we needed to start again. As a penciller I didn't always get fed by the competitions, so I had come prepared, and dug into my bag for an apple.

"How's that boy of yours going?" Judy asked me.

"I'm really happy with his progress. I'm not one to believe in luck, I'm rather someone who believes in building your own luck in life and with our horses. So for me it is about putting in the hard work to get to the best possible situation. I've been learning so much lately and applying these listening skills. It makes a huge impact to him and his energy.

I really have become curious about him and am trying hard to understand what he is telling me," I said.

"That sounds like you've got a great bond happening," Judy said.

"We do and he is really stepping up in everything he does. These new skills are also helping me in my daily life. They help me to live a healthy life, allowing me to acknowledge and cope with stress, expectation, and anxiety."

"My Maximilian was also one who gave me so much to think about. So I can understand what you're telling me," she said.

"We've been out jumping and he is getting much better. Very soon I'll be entering him into events such as this," I said smiling.

"You must. I can't wait to see you out here again."

"Neither can I," I replied.

We watched a couple of horses walking our way, and I scanned the sheet to see the next rider's number.

"No they aren't ours," I said.

"Oh goody, we can chat some more. I'm really keen to hear more about the work you are doing," said Judy.

"Sometimes I get a reality check from him and I need to stop and consider whether I am being present or not. Often I'm not, my mind is off thinking about work or something. He keeps reminding me that what is important when I am in his company is what I am doing right now. It's all about being accountable for being present and in the moment. When I am in the present moment, I can see improvement and our future gets better. When a connection is broken, I know I am the responsible person, and I am the one who needs to make the change," I said.

"You're right," came Judy's reply. "Plus when a horse is being what we call naughty there must be something bothering them. They don't wake up in the morning with the intention of annoying their owner. There is always a reason. If they are having difficulties digesting what you are asking them, you need to seek the reason why.

"Yes, this is the gold really, isn't it? This is where you start to get the answers," I said.

Judy continued, "I've always found that when horses are getting agitated, they are reacting. And when the rider takes the time to read their horse – ears, eyes, mouth, head level, the tail...it tells you lots of things. So many accidents could be prevented if people analysed and acted upon that information."

"Oops, we have a rider," I said looking across at the arena.

"Must get on," Judy said quickly "needs must."

"Yes, I look forward to continuing where we left off," I said as I opened my folder and checked the rider numbers.

We continued for the next couple of hours with only a brief break between riders, when Judy and I dashed off to the ladies.

After we had finished and we were waiting for the scorers to complete their work, Judy and I sat watching riders do their show jumping phase.

"Energy and body language are the two main ways a horse can

express themselves," Judy said as we watched a very vibrant horse go into the ring.

I saw a very distracted horse, and the rider sitting on him trying very hard to stay on. That horse didn't look like it wanted to be in that ring at all.

Judy continued, "When we look at the body language such as the pace, head, mouth, tail, ears, it tells the rider so much about the mental mindset of the horse. In this case, look at how he is not concentrating on the rider, and running at the fences. Goodness, I wouldn't want to ride him out on the course tomorrow."

"I bet that rider will trigger a spiral of energy to the horse. The horse is nervous, or the rider is nervous and together they are creating this storm of stress and anxiety, where neither is concentrating on the other; rather they are just trying to stay alive," I said.

"Scary," nodded Judy

As the horse crashed through the double and the whistle was blown to stop it whilst the fence was rebuilt, I turned to Judy and said, "Yep I agreed. I'm learning rapidly that the right kind of energy is one of the most important things, that triggers or calms your horse."

"The other day," I continued, "I was warming up for a small event and Bundy was super anxious. I'm not sure which one of us was the instigator, but when I recognised it, I stopped him in the warm up and asked him to stand. He didn't want to at first, yet as I asked him, still sitting in the saddle, I started to feel the earth come up to my feet. I felt the energy of the solid earth and the grounding it gave me."

"I took this energy across my body and as I did, Bundy Bear gave a sigh and blew out his nostrils. He stood still and I could feel his whole body relax. Once he was ready, I gathered up the reins and asked him to continue working. The test we rode after that was actually a winning test!"

Judy smiled at me and said, "When a horse doesn't trust and they are scared, what is the worst thing you can do?" I looked at her and waited for her to continue. "To get mad. If the rider chose to drop the energy and slow the breath, drop the shoulders, and give a presence of not being stressful, the horse will understand. Instead riders get angry and whip the horse and totally confuse it with heightened energy, often leading to disaster."

As the whistle blew to signify the course was ready for the rider to continue, we sat together watching them crash through another fence.

"Time to check with scorers, me thinks" said Judy. We both got up and walked away from the disaster unfolding in the jumping arena.

When I got home that evening I relayed to Tom the importance of the conversation I had had today with Judy. "I love these conversations we have. t really helps me to unpack what is happening with my horse, and sometimes it takes another rider to help me gain clarity." I said to him.

"Sometimes I actually know stuff, and surprise myself with what comes out of my mouth. That is gold for me. Other times I learn and contemplate" I said with a cheeky grin.

"Oh you know stuff aright," said Tom. I wasn't so sure, but nodded and smiled anyway.

EQUINE ASSISTED LEARNING

It is through these encounters that we recognise the interconnectedness of our experiences and the transformative power of human and animal connections.

I had learned from my time working with Bundy Bear that throughout his time of being harmed he held the belief that he could get through it. He had this unwavering hope that life would get better. A belief that someone would help him, and when he and I locked eyes that day in the warm-up ring, he knew I would help him.

Through my time of watching him and observing his behaviour I knew that Bundy Bear valued his 'herd' beliefs, and I suspected it came from his youth on the station. Just like wild horses, he knew the power of confidently communicating to the other, even though he had shut himself down from human communication. So over time in my stable he realised he could communicate with me and set about trying to communicate in the only way he knew. It took me many months before I realised he was sharing his message. As I didn't speak horse, and Bundy Bear didn't speak human, I had to learn to stop and watch and be still enough so I could listen and hear the message.

Sometimes I wonder if I am a slow learner, as I found myself missing the point, again and again. Was it my lack of focus, or my mindset and beliefs? Whatever the reason I recognised that I had to really learn to stop. Stop the noise in my head, and bring my focus to the task at hand. Through trial and error, I have been cheered on by Mr Bear and even through some failure, the mutual respect and belief we have for each other, has allowed me to see. Over time, we've built trust, respect and a strong relationship, each of us becoming a better being than we were before.

In his growing herd at my place, Bundy had taken up the role of being the leader. Initially, I didn't realise it, because it was so quiet. There was no expression of anger, or thrashing of hooves, or clashing of teeth, just a quiet acceptance that what he said, ruled. I noticed he would tilt his head slightly, or move an ear, and instantly the others would react. He oozed guru status from every pore. You couldn't see it, yet somehow you could feel it in the energy of the atmosphere. He was the sage to younger horses, the horse to follow, the leading light in our herd. Bundy Bear believed hat humans could listen to him, just like horses.

As I observed the situation, I realised that my act of listening could empower others to identify solutions to their problems or overcome obstacles that were impeding their progress. Bundy had previously demonstrated this ability to me multiple times, which helped me move forward with my own challenges.

As a manager of my team at work, I was often challenged with my lack of knowledge on how to move forward in my leadership. There were times when I would stop and think, how am I meant to respond to that, or what is my best move now?

My greatest teacher has always been Bundy. He constantly amazed me with the ways he helped me. Whenever I shared with others what he did while being handled or ridden, I would gain clarity and realise that the same scenario had occurred in my personal or professional life. Mr. Bear always provided me with the answers I needed. The next day, I would apply the lesson learned and my team would progress powerfully. Even during tricky situations in the boardroom or meetings I would ask myself, "What would Bundy do?" and his guidance would help me respond effectively. This practice was truly helpful.

When I saw this skill and the magic he had, I knew I needed to go back to school to learn how to share this ability with others so I could help them. I could see it could help business and leaders. I wanted to take leaders from the corporate world out into the paddock to be with the horses and to learn about themselves and their own leadership. I started to seek out information on how I could do this, and if anyone else was doing it. I quickly found that this practice was not widely known. Then one day I was reading an article in a magazine about a woman who practised Equine Assisted Learning with people and horses.

"Yay," I thought. "It actually does exist, it's called Equine Assisted Learning (EAL), and it helps people from all walks of life."

This article fuelled my passion to be a facilitator, to learn what there was to learn, so I could share with others. I was hooked.

For the next two years, I searched how I could train to learn the skills of facilitating EAL. What I found was that I needed to travel to the United States and spend a few weeks in the desert with the horses.

However, finally, I found a facilitator in Victoria, Australia who would help me to achieve this goal over a twelve month period. I booked in straight away. It was a long road ahead, yet one I so wanted to share and knew it would be fulfilling. I soon realised I had so much to learn about myself. The sessions were actually like therapy, yet longer, harder and more intense.

At one point whilst sharing a house with fellow students from all over Australia, I was the one who was having the psychotherapy session. It wasn't about me and the horses, and my ability to talk to them; it was all about me, and the way I behaved so that I could support my clients. There was so much for me to learn. So over the period of ten months I would attend these week-long camps of intense therapy. I would come home and practise and apply new skills, apply new learning and go back again. It was huge, and in the end it allowed me to see an even better side of myself, and ways to help others.

In my training, I was told that horses are therapeutic by virtue of just being a horse. They help to promote mindfulness and reconnect people to the present moment. This made total sense about the way Bundy Bear had been communicating with me. I had changed in the time I had been with him. I had become much more mindful. I was now more aware of my emotions and what I said or how I reacted with others, which ultimately had made life easier. I think maybe the therapy sessions whilst learning to be a facilitator of EAL, also helped me.

To conduct my EAL business I needed some more ponies to help build up my herd. So I went about finding some suitable ponies. I wanted ponies that were strong, and gorgeous, yet a bit smaller than Mr Bear. I found some gorgeous ponies that had come from the gypsies in England, they were called, "Gypsy Cobs." I hoped that the gypsies, as they were affectionately known, would have the same characteristics the wild horses did, in communicating, and the ability to inspire. The two girls I bought did, and with their foals they all helped people in different ways. Yet, regardless of their wonderful personalities, Mr Bear was always the star. In the sessions with Bundy Bear he would have total belief in the person and would listen to him. Whilst I am unable to vouch for every single person, I knew many people changed their life for the better because of his wisdom.

During his years at my stable we conducted many Equine Assisted Learning sessions with humans who were having a hard time in their life. Bundy Bear spread joyful magic amongst me and others. His energy was key to me becoming a facilitator, as I realised he had this amazing knowledge and skill in sharing information about my life to me, and that skill could help others too.

When setting up my business for EAL I offered this unique approach in a safe space, usually a yard or a small paddock. Each experience needed to be safe for both the horses and people. Sometimes it is the human emotions that affect the horses, other times it could be the handling or the client who puts themselves in danger. I remember one day, Wayne (a registered psychologist who has worked with me) and I were working with a group of kids who found it difficult to navigate life. There was a special program for them to join with other like-minded souls. That group arranged with us to come out to work with the horses.

I remember looking up during an activity and there was one of the boys climbing a huge tree. Oh my god, I thought, that is an insurance risk. I said nothing, but walked slowly over to just under the tree, and Bundy Bear followed me. We started to stand and gently interact. I was touching his nose, smelling his amazingness and talking gently to him. I could hear the boy moving about in the tree above me. My back was to the tree, so I couldn't see exactly what was happening, but I could hear movement coming closer. Within a few minutes he was on the ground wanting to talk to and smell the horse.

The whole approach to learning in this way is different and this experiential approach helps people to learn. They get away from their normal environment, they interact with gorgeous horses and ponies, and they might even learn something about themselves. Many people come out to our stables for the purpose of learning social-emotional skills, personal development, and professional development skills, but mostly they come to see what the horses can tell them.

My horses always interact with people without judgement or preconception. They just react to what is there at the time, and provide an open and honest interaction with all participants offering unique ways to help them. Being very intuitive the horses read body language, energy and the person's internal dialogue. The information given to each participant is often a greater awareness of living their life with choice.

At my place, there is never any riding for clients. It is always ground-based activities with the horses that allow me and my team to offer the participants insight into their all too familiar behaviour patterns. Patterns that have them feeling as if they are stuck in a rut which they can't get out of, regardless of what they do. The observations I made during the sessions, and communicated back to the clients added to their skills in everyday life - areas such as communication, self-esteem, focus, observation, respect, self-control, self-awareness and relationships.

One of the biggest areas I saw change in people was where participants had to modify or adapt their energy levels and actions in order to achieve the desired interaction with the horse. I would note how the modified behaviour would result in success, and we would discuss it afterwards. So often I would hear them say they had continued that new behaviour after they left the horse, and it had helped in their life.

Then of course there was the change in me, and my life. By doing the sessions, I was not only helping the participants, I was helping myself to understand at a body level. The more I facilitated, the more I practised what I preached, and my relationship with my horses, my husband and team almost sighed with relief. I was able to manage my emotions; I was aware of changes in my body and feeling more positive. I knew old fears could be and were removed, which helped me with moving through my feelings, especially the anger that would so often show itself at inopportune moments. As well as working with the horses in EAL, I listened to many mindful podcasts and meditations. This process allowed my unconscious mind to unlock its prison-like grip on me, and I could now move forward with calm and ease. The role of being a facilitator was important for me, and I needed to share the change. It worked on so many levels. I actually am very proud of the person I was becoming.

Another common reflection from participants was the awareness of the horse size, look, smell and feel. They loved being part of nature and out with the beautiful horses. They loved to touch them, smell them and watch them. So often people benefited from just hanging around in the space, and not being connected to a phone, and desperately searching for something on social media. For many, this allowed them to see a situation more clearly, or improve an outlook on life.

I worked with many people from differing backgrounds. Sometimes we would meet a participant once, other times we would see them over a period of time. It was always my aim to have people come over multiple times as I believe the repeated sessions resulted in longer term effects. Yet sometimes people just didn't want to come back, or their life changed and they couldn't visit again. In all cases I translated their experience with the horse through reflection. We would then, together look at ways of how that may apply to their life, or another person in their personal or professional life. I loved seeing the moments when the penny dropped, and they realised the horse had told them something really special.

One rainy Saturday in June, I had a session booked with a guy called Adam. I went outside to prepare to receive him. Rain was bucketing down and the wind was so strong it was blowing the rain sideways. It really wasn't pleasant. Regardless, I knew whatever the weather, we would go out and work with the horses. I prepared the herd, placing three horses into the space, including Bundy Bear who had a shed, just in case we needed to stand in it for protection.

Luckily the rains eased when it came time for him to arrive, and I even saw the sun trying to show its face. I smiled to myself and thanked the heavens for allowing us the time together. During the introduction to each other Adam explained that he was an actor, and that he wanted to work on areas of anxiety. I had already noticed he was tense in his shoulders, and I could see his jaw muscles twitching. I asked Adam to close his eyes and we did a grounding meditation together. I could see this really helped him to relax.

I invited Adam to introduce himself to all three of the horses, and gave him some instructions. As he walked over to where they were all standing, two horses started coming towards him. He stood still and waited. The two horses stopped and stood next to him. Rather than saying hello to them as I thought he would, he walked over to the one particular horse that had stayed away, Bundy Bear. As Adam walked towards where Bundy Bear was standing, Bundy walked away from Adam.

Adam marched resolutely towards Bundy Bear, outwardly displaying his determination to meet him. However, Bundy Bear continued to walk away and eventually headed towards the protective shed, as if engaging in a game of chase—man pursuing horse. Intrigued, I pondered the lesson Bundy Bear might be conveying. Just as Bundy Bear disappeared behind the shed, Adam abruptly stopped, his expression filled with confusion. Approaching him, I inquired about his current state of mind. Adam explained that he believed the horse didn't understand his intentions, and if it would only pause, he could greet it and bring happiness for them both. I probed further, asking Adam about his emotions regarding the situation. He responded, "I feel quite angry."

Wanting to explore his anger and its physical location, I asked Adam where he felt it in his body. After some thought he identified his chest as the location. To help him alleviate the tension, I guided Adam to take deep breaths and relax his hunched and tense shoulders. As he felt the tension dissipating, I continued to pose questions, encouraging him to delve deeper into his experience. Just then, one of the other two horses wandered over and positioned itself beside Adam. I inquired about the horse's presence and how it felt to have it stand by his side. Adam expressed gratitude and a sense of acceptance, describing it as a positive and comforting experience.

The process continued with me asking Adam what had drawn him to walk after the other horse that had seemed less interested. He expressed a need to be challenged, and wanted to engage with someone who seemed less accessible. He said that he genuinely was seeking something meaningful from these interactions and believed that overcoming the challenge would enable him to derive greater satisfaction. I felt this was important to explore, so I became curious and asked questions so that he could delve deeper and reflect into this aspect of himself. Eventually, I asked Adam, if he could identify other areas in his life where he perceived a similar pattern, where he consistently felt the need to prove himself. We discussed how this pattern occurs in other parts of his life. We then ended that session and went to have a drink and some refreshments.

After a small break I invited Adam to another task, and this time Bundy Bear came and stood right next to him. Again we went through facilitation and I set some tasks for Adam to achieve in the time away from us.

When he returned a couple of weeks later, Adam said the previous experience with the horses was not what he expected. In fact, he had found it rather challenging and intriguing. However, he said he had realised that the horses had helped him to identify a pattern in his life, and how he created anxiety. We worked on strategies to help him create new habits. Later, he reported back to me to say it had helped reduce his anxiety at work and in life.

The practice of equine assisted learning or facilitation is now booming across the world, and anyone of any age, background, ability or disability can benefit from such sessions with horses.

ACCOUNTABILITY

Accountability produces greatness.

I had planned a training session for my team at work which focused on the importance of being accountable for one's actions. I intended to present this topic during our weekly team meeting later that morning. I noticed that some team members had been blaming others or avoiding responsibility, so I felt compelled to address this issue. As I finished organising my notes and placing them into my leather folder, I realised that my hands were shaking. I was feeling nervous about sharing this information with my team.

"How odd," I thought as I walked down the hall to the room where we met. Before I entered I took a deep breath. "Be Bundy," I said inwardly.

"Hello everyone and thank you for all being here this week," I said as I found my seat and put my folder in front of me. Getting up to pour a coffee I looked around the room.

"Who is chairing today's meeting?"

Rodney raised his hand. "Awesome, are you ready then?" I asked.

"Yes," said Rodney

"OK, let's do this," I said breezily, breathing deeply and trying to placate the butterflies in my stomach as I walked back to my seat with my coffee.

Rodney went through the agenda and then got to my item.

I started, "Accountability is the skill for every relationship to thrive. It is when you are responsible for your actions. These relationships can be intimate partners, work colleagues, friends, and with your horse." I stopped and heard myself say that. "Well these amazing horses, do have to say their piece".

"I want to share with you today insights about how to work with your partner (we work on a mine site that requires people to be together at all times). The principles apply to many different areas in your life, especially at home with your life partner. BUT this is not about relationship counselling, it's about having a mentally safe workspace. It's not about one partner taking ownership, so that the others are happy. It's about both people, every employee taking ownership of the work they have been given. This accountability is a crucial part of efficiency in our workplace. I am here today to say that I have noticed some employee's lack of punctuality and their lazy and irresponsible behaviour. It doesn't go unnoticed. Our efficiency and safety is maximised when employees are accountable. It means taking ownership when we've accidentally done something wrong, hurt someone else, or let someone down.

When there is ambiguity in any relationship, workplace or at home, it creates an atmosphere where at least one person feels uncertain. When this happens neither person feels truly appreciated, and this can then cause safety concerns. Not being accountable for your actions is at the expense of our emotional and physical health, and the emotional and physical health of others.

Sometimes it also takes confidence, so that you can be accountable. When we really take ownership and then shift into action to improve things, it does a tremendous amount to build any relationship.

Being skilled at listening, taking supporting and opposing opinions into equal account when making decisions and being happy to honestly consider both, means you're being accountable and authentic."

I stopped speaking and looked at the room. No one said anything. So it was time to start asking some questions and getting their thoughts. The meeting continued for another hour.

Driving home that evening I pondered the meeting and how it went. As I went through their responses, I got thinking about my horses again. As a leader to my horses I am accountable for the questions I ask of them, and the responses I give to their answers. Just like my team every horse is unique, with distinct personalities and I need to respond based on their needs or preferences. I reflected upon my questioning technique today in the meeting. How I watched each person as they replied, just like I do with the horses. Only then did I respond with the next question or statement. It seemed to work, and I was amazed at how interesting that is. It is so similar to how I am now talking to the horses.

"Thank you once again, Mr Bear," I said out loud. "Once again you have helped me." The driver next to me caught my attention as she looked over and smiled a knowing smile. She gave a brief toot of her horn and sped off.

As I drove the familiar busy streets home, my thoughts drifted to how I tried to be accountable when I shared information with my friends. How I provided honest feedback and expected that in return. I wanted to learn about mistakes and issues when they arose, and sharing accountability when it was warranted. Our life is always a continuous journey of improvement. This also applied to when I worked with my horses and tried to establish what was happening, and reflect back to see how I could improve. This accountability I spoke about also means giving positive feedback and praise when it's deserved. Just like when I was working with Bundy Bear, I rewarded him for doing something well. I smiled as I thought about him taking pride in his accomplishments and how he so enjoyed being admired.

"Once again, Bundy Bear, you have me thinking about you constantly," I spoke aloud to the steering wheel. Suddenly, I noticed the another driver next to me watching, and I reacted with a surprised "oops," covering my mouth with my hand. I thought to myself, "Caught out again!"

I smiled and thought of how Mr B enjoyed being listened to, and how he loved his performances in the show rings and thrived on showing off.

Since learning how Mr B hadn't received any positive feedback prior to me rewarding him, I had been working on giving such positive feedback to others, to help them achieve their successes. Not that my team wants to show off, yet I felt it was important for their morale and trust in me as a person.

As I made a turn across the traffic and headed up the hill towards home, I reflected on the importance of being accountable for my own health and mental wellbeing. It is not only crucial for me but also for my family and team. I realised that it was my responsibility to remind my staff about the significance of being accountable for their eating habits, participating in healthy activities, exercising regularly, and developing a sense of mental stillness. All these things have a positive impact on the business. I parked in the driveway and thought to myself about tomorrow's plan to share these ideas with my team.

COUNSELLING WITH HORSES

These individuals appear as teachers in disguise, serve as catalysts for transformation and guide you along your journey of self-discovery.

The following day, a lady named Gigi, a prospective client, called to ask if she could bring her husband Randolph out to the horses for some relationship counselling. I agreed and set up the session date and time. I was mindful that it was a counselling session, so I called my business partner, Wayne, who is a registered psychologist, and asked if he could come out as well. Wayne had worked with me and the herd on many occasions, and he was a respected horseman.

The day came and I chose two of my young horses, both girls, and Bundy Bear to help the clients. The session was to last three hours. I released the horses in the pasture, and took the couple out to the paddock. Gigi was a small, very pretty lady wearing all white, and was draped in gold jewellery. On the outside she looked like she had her life together, a gorgeous looking man beside her, a successful business, and she had mentioned her luxury apartment overlooking the ocean. Randolph was a thick set, well built, handsome man. I smiled to myself about the white outfit. That won't stay clean for long around horses, I thought. My horses loved rolling in the dust, and when there was dust around they went right to it. This meant that the dirt would come off on people's hands if they touched the horses. It also was likely one or all three of them would nuzzle me, and their muzzle also carried dirt as it was constantly touching the ground.

Initially Gigi, was reluctant to be with the horses, yet as they were keeping their distance, I relaxed. Together, we began to focus on the goals for the session and I worked at a pace with which they both were comfortable. I explained to the couple how people are always the priority. I pointed out that they didn't need to be in the paddock; if they liked they could engage with the horses from the outside. They both agreed they would prefer to be inside with them all.

During one of the sessions I asked the couple to take ten minutes to observe the horse interactions. I asked them to move around the paddock, where they were comfortable, whilst Wayne and I would observe them, and be there to ensure safety.

As they walked out to the paddock, the couple separated. What both Wayne and I noticed was that Gigi went to the girls who were both standing in the middle of the paddock. As I got closer to them, they both lay down on the ground with their feet folded beneath them. They both had their heads up, but were relaxed. Gigi sat down on the grass and patted them both. It was a beautiful sight to watch, even if it wasn't so good for the white clothes!

Randolph strode off towards Bundy Bear, who was standing some way off. When Randolph got to where Mr Bear was he walked purposely around him. Mr Bear appeared to be solid, having lifted his head high and almost appeared to be looking down on Randolph. Then after a moment it appeared that both man and horse were doing a dance. Both of them took small steps around each other. At one point Randolph stood with his hands on his hips, just staring at Mr Bear. He in turn just stood and looked back. It appeared Mr Bear had something he really wanted to share, yet he was doing it in a quiet, determined way. Both Wayne and I noted that there had been no physical contact between the two. Once Randolph was done, he walked back to where we were standing, and we noted that he didn't go past the girls at all.

When they both returned, I asked them what they noticed about their behaviour and interactions between the horses. They took the opportunity to talk about the individual horses, what they had observed as they met the horses and anything they wanted to share about their mannerisms. This was then related to human interactions as a couple, responsibility and safety.

The session continued with similar smaller sessions, where the couple would be asked to do something with the horses and then would be asked questions. In these sessions, there is no right or wrong answer. It is whatever the person is willing to share.

The facilitators design these discussions to gain insights into the personalities of the individuals involved. They use questions to encourage clients to share their problems or related issues during the session. The information gathered serves as a starting point for the clients to implement changes within themselves. Using this process, the facilitators can assist in achieving meaningful and visible changes in the couple's life.

During these discussions, Randolph, the husband, clearly expressed his belief that Bundy Bear was a bully and behaved in an unacceptable manner by pushing his weight around. Despite Wayne and I never observing Bundy push Randolph around, Randolph remained adamant about his belief. To explore this further, the sessions were altered to see if Randolph felt the same way with other horses, but he did not share his feelings. We discussed Randolph's feelings about Mr Bear with him, but he continued to blame the horse.

By the end of the sessions he said he'd had enough and wanted to leave. Gigi loved all of my sessions, and said she felt at total peace with all the horses, especially the girls. It was displayed by the way all the horses relaxed around her. We noted that they did not do too much together as a couple, even though we suggested it.

I was saddened to have someone say that about my beloved Mr

Bear. I wasn't used to anyone not liking him. Yet, I knew I had to be professional and accept what was presented to me. Wayne and I discussed what had happened, and sought feedback on the session. As practitioners we don't lay judgement, yet they questioned if something underlying was happening in the relationship of the couple.

When I called Gigi to see how things were a couple of weeks later, she was breezy and said everything was just fine. She told me, "I really liked the session, but we're busy with work and I can't see that we can return in the near future." Gigi was a very successful entrepreneur, and she was often travelling around the globe. There was nothing more to do.

It wasn't until some twelve months later that Gigi called me. On the call she explained she had put her husband on a restraining order, and that he had been quietly bullying her, with the intent to harm her life. She had no idea it was happening, as it was underhand. At the time of booking in for the session, she knew something was up, but couldn't put a finger on it. She knew of the horses having a powerful way with humans, and hoped that it would bring insight. She told me that she did leave the session with an inclination; however, whilst she wanted to discuss it with him, in the end, to keep the peace, she never mentioned the session again to him. Randolph was adamant it was the horse; love prevailed and she endured many months more of abuse.

Her life had been at risk, and she said to me, "One day I woke up to it. I wanted to thank your horses, as it was clear that the black and white horse knew exactly what was going on." She said, "I should have listened to the feedback on the day. Yet I didn't want to and negated it. Sadly he was right, and I learnt the truth after much more abuse."

RESPONSIBILITY

Taking personal responsibility is an empowering choice to make, so that we live with integrity, authenticity, and purpose. The choice liberates us from the constraints of circumstance.

Taking responsibility for your actions never arises when everything is okay. Yet as humans, we make mistakes, and sometimes things don't go as planned. Taking responsibility means that you play a part in every situation or experience and have some degree of responsibility over the outcomes or consequences of that situation. It is a bit like being accountable, but different. Being responsible means that when we make a mistake or something doesn't go as planned, you don't twist the facts, blame others, make excuses, or flat out lie. Instead, you acknowledge there is a problem, identify your role in it, and think of a way to reduce the chances of it happening again. This in itself is an opportunity to learn and grow.

Reflecting on all the wisdom I gained from Bundy Bear, I began to contemplate my training methods. It became clear to me that I didn't want to sacrifice the essence of the real horse by solely focusing on dressage or pushing for constant competition. I cherished his inner spirit, his innate joy, his desire to please, and his yearning to explore and enjoy life.

Right from the moment Bundy arrived at my place, I noticed how his competitive endeavours had drained him emotionally and physically. Week after week, he tirelessly competed. While some horses thrive in a goal-oriented, competition-driven lifestyle, many others don't. They become disheartened, withdrawn, and their mental well-being lags behind their physical capabilities. Perhaps the stress of constant competition took its toll on them.

I couldn't ignore these observations, and it made me question the impact of competition on a horse's overall well-being.

I held a significant responsibility to provide my horses with a lifestyle that served their equine nature. I recognised that compassion entailed responsibility, respect, loving-kindness, and a sincere willingness to support. I constantly asked myself a crucial question: "What choice would be most compassionate for the horses and everyone involved?"

Posing this question takes courage, and I discovered that it evoked some intriguing emotions in others too. I anticipated truthful responses and a readiness to take action if required, presenting an opportunity for constructive transformation.

As I spent more time learning about myself and the horses, I noticed that I began to grant the horses and those around me more freedom. By paying attention to my emotions and identifying the underlying needs, I was able to fulfil those needs and foster better understanding and connection. What I gained from my experiences with the horses translated into a valuable skill that I was able to apply in other areas of my life.

I learned to communicate with horses through my emotions. While humans often don't consciously pick up on the energy of emotions, horses can be affected by them. When Bundy Bear brought this to my attention, I became aware of what was happening inside myself and was able to make a choice. The more I listened to my emotions, the better I understood how past wounds and traumas affected not only myself but also the horses and others.

I realised that I had a choice in how I reacted to my emotions and that I didn't have to be troubled by feelings of jealousy or ego that can lead to competition between people. I also realised that the answers to my problems weren't always outside of myself and that self-reflection was an important process.

Like horses, people may avoid taking responsibility for reasons ranging from laziness to fear of failure or feeling overwhelmed.

I had been working with Bundy for over three years. I was finding it to be a wonderful experience and loved the relationship. Throughout this time, I found that how I showed up and behaved was the key to any of the training. However what I did initially was to fall into the 'be nice and mindful' mindset too deeply. When I worked Bundy in dressage, improvements happened very slowly. He was strong-willed and still showed me his insecurity. It wasn't until I finally got my trainer to ride him that I saw where a lot of the problem was. I was not being the leader anymore. I realised he needed firm guidance in his training.

When Bundy was held responsible for his actions, attitudes and movement, he became a different horse. He actually calmed down and became happier. He found confidence and security when I was showing him the boundaries.

When I wasn't firm but instead responded with a "maybe that's right," my inaction allowed him to take control. I learned that there's a fine line between being too passive and too forceful. To have a successful ride and interactions with my horse, I needed to have clear intentions for every second of our time together.

If my horse wasn't responding to a request he had been trained to know, I needed to be very clear that his response wasn't what I wanted. Then, I would softly communicate to him through aids, saying, "this is what I'm asking." By having clear intentions backed up with clear requests, I was able to communicate effectively with my horse. However, this was not an easy process. Working with a horse requires patience, persistence, and clarity.

There is always a challenge with being able to give choice and finding a way to build trust. I wanted to be the leader of the herd so that they knew they were safe and we could have fun together. We needed to get to a point where the horses shared the decision making responsibilities, because they felt safe to do so. My aim was to get them to a point of being calm and exhibiting the ability to trust me, the process and the environment.

Being completely present was key. So I started with a short session, where I could keep my focus, paying attention to Bundy. This way Bundy would become secure and confident enough to act in partnership. I found when I became more assertive and raised my expectations for my horse's performance, it improved. I realised I needed to continue to be firm and fair, while riding more precisely. Firm, fair and consistent was the best and most balanced approach.

The key to responsibility is to recognise what happened, not blame, and understanding that you need to take your own responsibility. Consider your own behaviour and the consequences of that behaviour. Recognise that you are in control, and that control will allow you to develop self-respect and have the respect of others. Taking responsibility defines your true character.

BELIEFS

We are what we think.
All that we are arises with our thoughts.
With our thoughts we make the world.
- Buddha

Beliefs → Behaviours → Become.
    I had been doing some research on beliefs for my work, and I found a TED talk that Rick Warren gave in 2006 where he said, "Your worldview determines everything else in your life…what we believe determines our behaviour, and our behaviour determines what we become in life."

I then read James Clear's Atomic Habits book where he said, "The basic idea is that the beliefs you have about yourself can drive your long-term behaviour." He was essentially saying that you become what is formed from your habits, and every belief, including those about yourself, is learned and conditioned through experience.

So your beliefs become your behaviours or habits and that is how you become who you are. And the more you repeat that behaviour, the more you reinforce and validate who you are.

These beliefs are framed by your values.

> *"Your beliefs become your thoughts,*
> *Your thoughts become your words,*
> *Your words become your actions,*
> *Your actions become your habits,*
> *Your habits become your values,*
> *Your values become your destiny."*
>
> \- Mahatma Gandhi

My beliefs have played a huge part in my life. In fact, these convictions in my mind, made everything I thought true, and I accepted that these things were real to me. This I now know, had kept me playing a smaller game than I could have. There were times when I thought everyone believed the same thing as me, yet I found out through working with my horse (and myself) that they don't. I learned that each of us is shaped by so many other factors.

I've also come to realise that we possess both limiting and empowering beliefs, and they operate like switches that are unconsciously turned on or off throughout the day. When the switch is off, we harbour the belief that we are incapable of achieving certain things, thus imposing limitations on ourselves. Conversely, when the switch is on, we embrace the belief that we are capable and empowered. It is this empowering belief that propels us toward the life we desire. Through introspection, I've become aware of my unconscious habits, which are essentially the ingrained beliefs that operate without conscious thought. Once I began recognising these habits, I gained the ability to make positive changes and take control of them.

This awareness allowed me to see how these beliefs were negatively impacting my life. My mind was becoming stronger each day, and I knew I had the power to change my situation. The best change always starts from within, not from outside. I have all the resources I need for change within me. When I believed that I was capable, competent, and deserving I practiced, and acted like the goal was mine; I noticed opportunities that could help me get there. Ultimately I achieved the goal.

When I started to jump Bundy Bear, I wondered if I would ever get him to jump in a competition again. In fact, at one time I started to believe that he was ruined for life. When he kept stopping at fences, and knocking rails, I wondered if he was too damaged to move through it. Then one day my instructor told me, "it looks like you don't believe he can do it". Initially, I was miffed when I heard this, and just kept on riding, not responding to my instructor. Later though, after I had unsaddled, I started to reflect on what I was doing and how I was reacting to my horse as he approached the fences.

That was a huge realisation for me. I went home and talked to Tom about it. As the conversation progressed, I knew my instructor was right. I had started to believe Bundy couldn't jump, so I had been keeping him safe, and allowing him to stop. I was allowing him to make decisions, rather than pushing through and being confident.

So, once again, I went back to practicing changes to my habitual way of thinking. I kept up my practice of a gratitude journal, and mindfulness meditation. These practices helped me notice and appreciate the good in life especially with my horse. These practices enabled me to break free from unproductive, negative thoughts and embrace a more constructive mindset.

I started to set clear intentions for how I wanted to respond to Bundy when I jumped him. This was the hard bit, yet gradually I aligned my behaviour with those intentions. The recognition that my beliefs were limiting their success made a huge impact on Bundy Bear and their results. Not only did it change the results with him, it also flowed out into my personal life. Once again, Bundy Bear had helped me become more aware of who I was, and how I thought.

After a few months it was time to start taking him out to the competitions. I had a fierce, inner competitor that I had suppressed for a long time, and it now was itching to come out. Knowing we were ready to start competing again it influenced my every move. I knew that competition in itself can make me very self-centred, if I let it. I had experienced in the past where my thoughts became consumed with the need to win. At that time, my enjoyment had gone out the window, and I was ready to walk away from something I loved. Not this time though.

I entered him in events that he could handle, and when he said he was ready to jump the next height we would give it a go. I entered events where he would be doing what he used to do; dressage, show jumping and cross country. I kept my personal passion alive and was aware of unique, specific reasons for riding and helping me with horses. This built psychological strength and positive energy like nothing else. The passion and dedication helped Bundy Bear and fuelled our love for going together. It was an extremely powerful force that helped me to reach my goals, sustain effort and meet my riding challenges.

Within two years of going back to jumping he was soft and happy and loved competing. It took us time to gather that momentum, to build up that trust and to really feel that we were partners. When my horse would talk to me, it was amazing. No words could describe that feeling nor the love of the relationship. This is what motivated me.

We entered competitions with huge classes. Yet, as the partnership grew, so did our results. We would show ourselves in all our glory, sometimes we would struggle, we always had fun and many times we had small wins. I rode with the idea that riding was what fulfilled me and being better at riding was what kept me going. We won many ribbons, and rugs, and I felt successful. There is always more to learn, yet seeing my horse with one of his many embroidered rugs with the event name and class that we won together, is a huge thrill.

Bundy was finally happy in himself and what he did.

INTROVERT VERSUS EXTROVERT

Understanding one's unique strengths and contributions, provides a more inclusive and harmonious environment.

On a lovely spring Sunday in September, I was down at the Equestrian Centre where we were preparing for a dressage competition. I was warming up outside in an arena with Bundy - just the two of us together. It was a beautiful day, the sun was shining, yet the arena was cool. I was really enjoying Bundy Bear and the connection we had. Suddenly he stopped dead in his tracks, and stared at another horse that had walked in the arena. The fact that another horse had entered was nothing new, so I didn't think that was the reason for his response. There was nothing odd about the rider, the horse or no one else who was walking past. So I couldn't work out the cause of his discomfort. Then it dawned on me. The horse was a big beautiful black and white horse. Just like Bundy Bear! He was terrified of the other horse's colour. I imagined he had never seen another coloured horse, or the sight of the horse reminded him of something from his past.

Whatever the reason, he continued to move around the horse like it was going to kill him, and he soon became very agitated. It was this same behaviour I had witnessed in other horses as they saw us when warming up. I had to move him away quickly, or the dressage test he was about to undertake, would be ruined.

Not long after this event, I attended a clinic with Bundy Bear where they had mirrors in the indoor arena. The minute he saw his reflection in the mirror he stopped dead and stared. This time he wasn't scared, but he didn't want to move. He wanted to look, to appreciate himself, and the colour he was. That was a changing point for him and his attitude.

He became comfortable with his looks, and quickly realised how gorgeous he was.

Over a coffee with Hayley, I was telling her about this and how I found it fascinating.

Hayley said, "You know Bundy Bear is an extrovert?"

"Pardon?" I said surprised. I was an introvert, and needed time being by myself, and hadn't actually thought about my horse being an extrovert. "Oh wow! Of course" I said. "Yes he certainly loves to be with others, and to show off!" In my head, I ticked off the times I had witnessed him displaying these behaviours. "Sometimes I think extraverts are so in your face," I said to Hayley.

"Introverts or extroverts are not right or wrong – simply different," came Hayley's reply.

"Yes, I get that, I just hadn't correlated the two, and was reflecting on my own reactions," I replied.

Bundy Bear was a typical extrovert. He thrived in large social activities. He got his energy from outside of him, the environment, others, being in exciting surroundings, and being active. He loved getting attention from others.

Now that he had overcome his anxiety, he loved nothing more than announcing his arrival. As he walked off the float, he'd look around, throw his head in the air and standing tall; as if saying to everyone "I'm here. I know you've all been wanting to meet me!" And sure enough his fan club of pony clubbers (seriously they would arrive from anywhere!) would come over to him and pat him, and say how wonderful he is.

His fan club loved his colouring and always reacted to his presence, his *je ne se quoi* - *that something you couldn't fathom about Bundy*. He loved all the pats, the cuddles, and comments like, "Oh isn't he gorgeous", "I love this horse," "he is beautiful." It soon became apparent he would look for these compliments. I'd watch him swing his head and bottom as we walked to a warm up ring. I'd always have him on a long rein, so he was free to move his head; however he liked. He'd look around, ears pricked, and sometimes even nicker at someone.

He was the typical extrovert where he liked to be out and about socialising, and feeding off the energy of his external environment and others. It started to make total sense to me. He lapped it up. Even though he loved the feeling of dirt on his body, he loved nothing more than the day before a show where he would be washed (three times!). He'd have his toes cleaned, and polished, his whites totally washed and cleansed with purple wash, and his tail would be soaked and scrubbed. Then he'd be plaited up ready for the competition. He would stand there all day if someone was preening him! He even started to improve his performance in the ring after he had received some attention from admirers.

Being an introvert, I usually enjoy thinking, reading, writing and being in nature. I love being alone, and just being, and it is this space where I find my energy, where I recharge. I can be an extrovert when I choose to, I can party and be in crowds, but afterwards I always need time and space to recharge and I do that by being alone.

Mostly, I prefer to spend time with small, intimate groups where I can relate to others on a deeper level. Hence, the need to have quiet coffees with my girlfriends, and long rides out in the bush. I get my energy from time alone, rather than from social stimulation.

Dealing with an extroverted individual can be draining for me, as they tend to talk incessantly with boundless energy and an insatiable desire to keep going. Having a horse with a similar temperament was often exhausting as well. He would always seek the spotlight, demanding attention, and while he held the centre stage, I still had to engage in conversation alongside him.

There are many things I have learnt through being with my horses, and especially Bundy Bear. They provide me with a sense of being and of happiness. I have huge gratitude to the horses for allowing me to realise this, and to the feeling of being held.

As a young adult, I didn't get much of this in my life, and as a leader I spent most of my time being there for others, and this became very draining. So being with the horses is something very special. When I started realising this, I knew that I was at peace with the horses; they allowed me to gain strength and resilience. In turn, this allowed me to become a better person without feeling drained.

I learnt that it's the little things right now that matter. I recognised that in order to achieve large goals, when I set smaller more attainable goals they were easier for the team to achieve.

I enjoyed the way I felt around horses, especially Mr Bear. With him I was beginning to feel enveloped in his state of peace and calm. I rode him to merge with this body of the horse that is so much larger than me. I wanted to feel that my heart was at one with his enormous heart. It was deep.

A need to communicate love and affection to Mr Bear and to know without a doubt that I was loved back.

As he became comfortable in his stable, and being ridden out and about. I noticed his sense of humour, his strong curiosity and a huge sense of play. I could see that he was confident around me and I was supporting him and when he was distressed. His exceptional mind showed he was here to serve, and he loved his job. It seemed now that he didn't need to worry all the time about his life, he was comfortable to show this side again. The relationship is based on mutual respect and trust. He blossomed with well-being.

The relationship was built on having a two- way dialogue of listening and responding.

A continual learning of deeper skills for communication through contact, energy, alignment, deeper horse listening and keeping the joy are key to the success of the relationship.

This positive energy can also be nurtured by surrounding yourself with encouraging people who offer respect, kindness and honesty.

The journey was never ending. Accepting the mistakes I made was hard at the beginning; however it became part of my daily life, and business process, to reflect and have the awareness to understand what I don't know and what we need to do. There were times when I worried about making mistakes yet I knew that if it felt right then I would make a decision and stay with it. I would watch to see if it worked, and I was mindful that everyone else knows more than I did.

I wanted to walk my own path and to ensure I was only influenced by people I respected and who showed both humility and kindness.

Just like Bundy Bear enjoys the security of knowing I am making powerful decisions, I also enjoy the benefits of becoming more responsible for myself. And this is reflected in every dimension of my life. This horse has helped me to find deeper inner strength. When I came from a place of anxiety and expectation it wore me down, and affected my relationships with my family, with friends and at work! This continual nurturing has enhanced my self-worth, self-love and self-motivation and allows me to reconnect with my truest emotions.

My new discipline of becoming more aware of my thoughts, body language and breathing communicates with the horse in a most profound way; It is a way of sharing the ability to connect with his world. I use these tools in all aspects of my life, and they have helped me in so many different ways. Being in the 'here and now' and allowing my mind to just stay in the present moment, has allowed me to learn the personal power of just feeling, being and allowing. It has helped my mental health, and the way I am with others. It's helped my leadership capability and my relationships. Even though it is a continuous journey, I work hard to let go of stressful thoughts of achieving, perfecting and the demanding expectations of my normal lifestyle. I continue to reflect on what the horses share with me and how that is also occurring in my work life. There is always a message for me.

Just the other day, I was called by my neighbour who had seen my horse galloping around in their paddock. I ran over to the paddock and couldn't see anything that might have set them off; however, I could unmistakably see both horses galloping frantically around the paddock, and snorting. I was concerned they might hurt themselves, by going through a fence, or galloping wildly over rough terrain and damaging a leg, hoof, or shoulder. As I looked on, they were in full flight and it appeared to me that they were fearful of something. Their ears were back and they were running hard.

At first, I felt a slight 'panic!' as two large horses when they are fearful is very daunting, especially when you are in the paddock with them. Then I decided I needed to be a leader, so I started to breathe calmly and deeply. I walked through their gate and stood. I started to lower my energy to slow down the horses. I slowed my breath and dropped my shoulders, I wanted to regain their trust in me and to let them feel safe. I chatted away soothingly to them and remained standing but still, being mindful of calmness, as if nothing was happening, and there was absolutely nothing to worry about.

Instantly, I felt the energy calming, and then they both galloped up to where I stood and stopped. They stood quivering, yet calm. I watched as the two horses stood puffing and sweat dripped from their bodies, their bellies heaving with each breath. As I stood watching the horses tune in to me, I heard them blowing down through their nostrils several times. That was what I was waiting for. That recognition that all was calm. At this point they walked up to me and asked to be comforted, which I did. I reached over and calmly stroked Bundy's neck whilst talking soothingly to them. I behaved as a leader in the wild would do - stand still and calm, and then the herd will go back to grazing.

I wanted to walk them back to their stables, and whilst I would normally walk them alongside me, this time I felt I needed a head collar, just in case they got excited again. Plus, we were in the paddock close to the road, so I didn't want them going down that way. So I made the decision to run back to the stables and get a couple of head collars. I asked the horses to stand and relax whilst I ran back. As I ran down the path I slowed and turned back to look at them. Both horses were watching me. They continued to stand and wait. When I returned - some 3 minutes later - they were still standing, looking, waiting for me.

I haltered them and led them back into the stables. Both were content to be with me and heading to their place of safety; yet still a little agitated. As we walked to the stables I checked in with them several times to see if they were choosing to listen to me, and calm themselves. This in itself helped them to release their energy and bring them back to a place of safety. By the time we were in the stables, they both were back to being the placid horses they are normally.

I realised that the bond of trust between both of my beautiful big horses was growing daily, and even in a time of panic, they chose to listen.

This not only happens in the paddock, it also happens at work. I suddenly realised I was leading now. I am a leader. It was quite an emotional moment for me!

INTERSCHOOL COMPETITION

Beware, for those who seek to fulfil their own unfulfilled dreams or desires through living vicariously shall only find tears and sorrow in their path.

Sunday evening, just before dinner, I was scrolling through social media and saw an invitation for horse owners in Western Australia to allow their horse to be ridden by an interstate school child for the upcoming interstate school competition. The Australian Inter-school Championships attracts children aged 5-18 years old and has more than 2,000 school based competitors, family, friends and supporters from right around the country. It is a big event, and one where children need to qualify to ride. Inter School comprises a competition and educational pathway for young athletes to participate in equestrian sport during their primary and secondary school years. This year the event is in WA and as such riders would be mostly coming without their horses. That means they would require to borrow horses for their events.

The advert read that they were looking for horses to do Dressage, Jumping, Eventing and Show Horse. Bundy Bear was going fantastically, and I thought why not? I decided to discuss it with Tom before I made any final decision. Later that night I brought it up, and he agreed it would be a wonderful opportunity to share Bundy's talents with someone. To be honest, I was pretty excited about the prospect of someone else riding him, now that he was in this amazing way of being. I walked over to my computer, and emailed the organising committee, attaching his photo.

The following week I was sent an email asking a few questions like: a) What height had he jumped? I responded: training up to 120cm in the past.

b) What height was he currently competing in? My response: We've just moved up from 80cm eventing at 95cm having completed three events at this height.

c) What is the horse's height? My response: 16.3hh.

Some six weeks later, I was emailed back and told a rider had been selected to ride my horse. The email said what she was competing in but it really didn't make any sense to me, as the competition categories were not ones I was used to seeing. I had entered him thinking he would be evented, but it turned out he was just doing show jumping rounds. I accepted however, that the committee knew what they were doing and all would be fine. It was an official committee right? And they had riding experience and the welfare of all horses in mind, I thought to myself.

A week before the rider arrived, I got an emailed with her name, and that she was coming from Geelong, Victoria. Crystal and her family would be coming to WA in early June. I was excited that Bundy Bear would be getting to compete in this competition, and that I could watch him.

It was Tuesday afternoon when Crystal and her family arrived to meet Bundy Bear. Crystal was a medium built rider, dressed in designer rider attire. She glowed and sparkled. We decided that before we went out to the horses we would share a cup of tea. Over the tea and a banana and chocolate chip cake I had baked that morning, I heard that Mum, Gloria worked as a horsemanship instructor at the local Technical College. That gave me confidence that they knew what they were doing. Her father, Samuel, was in insurance, and it appeared he did whatever his wife and daughter asked him to do. Tom was keen to share the story of Bundy Bear with them, and wanted them to know that this was one special horse, and he was to be treated with the respect he deserved. They agreed they would, and they told me a couple of times that they knew what they were doing. We learned that Crystal was 15 years old and in year 10 at school. Gloria said to me, "she is a great rider, and really knows what she is doing," as we walked to the yards.

I have been told before that I trust too quickly, so I tried to feel into my body to find if I was doing it again and trusting them too quickly. I felt the stories they told me resonated, and my gut wasn't protesting, so I believed them. I was excited at having my horse being ridden by someone else.

The competition wasn't for another ten days, so Crystal and her mother were staying in Western Australia, so she could practice on Bundy Bear. Her father was flying back to Victoria to work until the event when he would fly back. When we walked to the yard Crystal met Bundy Bear, but she decided she didn't want to ride him as she was tired from the trip. We arranged for her to come back the next morning so she could ride before they went shopping for the day.

I woke up early the next morning to clean my saddle and bridle, ready for Crystal and her ride on Bundy Bear. I was keen to make sure everything fitted correctly and they knew how I wore his gear. Whilst I knew many riders liked to strap down horses' mouths to keep them shut, and stop them from resisting the bit, or held their heads down with martingales, or used gear that was ill fitting, I was very conscious he could be the most comfortable time possible. I always rode him in a nose band, which was supportive, but not so tight that it hurt him. I never wore any straps that were used to cover a rider's weakness. It was important to me that his gear was well cared for and comfortable at all times. Even his body was given regular massages to help his muscles to work through the pressures of competing. For me, having a happy horse meant it was about a whole wellness program, including his diet, nutrition, feet, and gear - not just being ridden.

Crystal and her mother Gail arrived the next day and I took them through my procedures. Gail was very dismissive, which I put down to nerves, or excitement, or maybe she knew it all and didn't need me telling her. I thought of what she taught at the college and realised I was probably preaching to the converted. However, I continued to show them how I fitted all his gear, and shared the amount of space between his head and the bridle, and noseband, to make sure they understood my viewpoint. I also didn't like wearing spurs, as I explained to them that when I had first got him, I remembered wearing spurs on my boots, and he had taken off during an event. He was uncontrollable, and I had put it down to the spurs. Since I had removed them, he had always done as I asked, and I never felt the need to wear them again. He didn't need it. He jumped freely and enjoyed it when we went out.

When Crystal mounted him I took them out to my arena and asked her to warm him up. I watched as she trotted him and cantered him around. Once I felt she had warmed him enough I put up some jumps and asked her to jump them. The first two he jumped clear, then the next one he refused.

"Gosh, that's odd" I said to Gail, "he never does that."

"Have another go Crystal," I called across the arena. She turned him around and cantered towards the jump. Bundy Bear jumped it, but not in his normal flowing way. I didn't know what to do, so I continued to stand in the arena and watch as he stopped, then jumped, then stopped, then jumped. Gail stood on the sidelines and didn't say anything. I was keen for Crystal to do well with him, and I knew he was capable, but I had no understanding as to why he was stopping.

Gail said to me, "perhaps if you left the arena he would be happier. You know maybe he doesn't want to disappoint you."

"Good point," I said "Maybe you are right." So I walked away and hid behind a tree, so that I could still see him, but he wasn't looking at me. I stood watching them and what I saw was him jumping every jump. There was not a time he refused.

I came back as they unsaddled him as I wanted to talk it over. I wanted to try and understand, and to make sure he was being treated well. Gail assured me everything was fine as she took off his saddle, "We are fine, you don't need to be here. We can come and get him, saddle him and ride. That way you're not distracted, and he jumps."

Reluctantly, I agreed and walking to the tack room said, "So if you come every day, I can leave his saddle and gear here for you to use."

"Okay," said Gail "are you fine with us saddling him, or do you want to?"

I wasn't sure, but felt that if he was not jumping to support me, then maybe I didn't need to be around him to put his gear on. "No that's OK," I said "you can saddle him if you are happy to do that."

"Yes, that's great," said Gail as she smiled at Crystal.

Over the next few days, I watched them come and go to ride Bundy Bear. I watched from a distance and saw him jumping his fences. It appeared everything was going well. Each day, I would walk over after he had been ridden and ask how things were, and they both said all was fine.

"Hi Amanda," Gail said on Wednesday morning. "Could you float Bundy Bear down to the State Equestrian Centre tomorrow so that we can get settled in?"

"Doesn't the competition start on Friday?" I asked as I leant on the stable railing.

"Yes, but I want Crystal to have a day beforehand to get to know the space and make sure Bundy Bear was happy with the grounds. He will be stabled for the four days at the Centre, and his first event is early Friday morning.

I was taken aback. This had not been mentioned before. "Well, I have a work meeting in Welshpool at 9am tomorrow, so that would be inconvenient." I thought a bit more and said "I could come home early and take her there at about 3pm if that works?"

"Oh no, you can't do this to us, we need him there tomorrow morning." Said Gail.

Her response was a surprise, and I had no idea this was coming.

"Well, let me see what I can do," I said as I walked off to get my diary. As I walked I considered the situation and realised I could possibly go earlier with Bundy Bear and the float, leave the float at the Equestrian Centre and then collect it on my way back from my client. I knew my client meeting would take about five hours, so that meant it wouldn't be too hard, and I'd probably miss the peak hour traffic.

By the time I got back to the stables, Gail was leading the unsaddled Bundy Bear back to his stable. "Gail" I said "I think I can do it if I leave early. Would that be suitable for you?"

She took off his head collar, and closed his paddock gate behind him. "Sure, what time do you think you'll be there?"

"About 7am and then I can unhook the float and unload all of his gear."

"Ok, we'll meet you there then" Gail said.

The next morning I got up super early and packed two sets of clothes; one to be around my horse and his gear, and the other to wear to my client's workplace. I had already packed the float and it was full of rugs, feed, feed bins, riding gear, and stable gear such as a poop scoop, rack for cleaning the stables, and water buckets that would be needed for the four days of the competition. Each item had been marked with his name, so that it wouldn't go missing.

As we drove down the hill to the Equestrian Centre, I was in a good mood and eager for what lay ahead for Bundy Bear, and also very pleased the traffic was light. Even though it was early in the morning, as I entered the equestrian centre there was plenty of activity. Floats were pulling in, horses were being walked around and riders were getting coffee from the coffee van. I drove around to the back of the centre and looked for a park amongst all the other cars. I needed to find a place where I could safely leave the float and know that I could hook it back up again later that day. In the end, I found a small space, and backed into it. I got out of the car and walked around to let the back ramp down to unload Bundy Bear. He whinnied inside the float, calling out to the other horses. Odd I thought, he never does that.

I let down the ramp, and he walked off with his head high in the sky. As I started walking to the stable area I noticed Crystal coming towards me.

"Hi, we're over here," she said, pointing to a row of stables. I handed her Bundy Bear's lead rope and walked alongside them both.

"We've got two stables," she said "one for him, and one for our gear."

"Oh that's great," I said "as we have lots of stuff to leave here"

Once he was in his stable I walked back to start unloading the float. It took about twenty minutes before it was all done, and then I looked at the time and realised I needed to get changed and get to my client.

"I have to get going," I said, as I started walking back to my car. "What time will you be riding him?"

Crystal looked up at her Mum with a questioning look, "Mum?"

"Oh around 3pm I should think," said Gail.

"That's perfect. I should be able to see you ride when I come back to get the float. I'll see you then," I said as I rushed back to the float, to get changed. Once changed I started the journey to my clients. I felt into my body, it was telling me something, but I wasn't sure what. I wondered if it was anticipation, or nerves, or maybe I was just keen to get the client work done satisfactorily.

The day went quickly and at 1230pm I had finished everything I needed to do.

"So I can leave now, Jim" I told my client "you know what to do from now on?"

"Yes that's fine Amanda, we'll be grand" he said in his Irish accent.

I started my drive back to the State Equestrian Centre anticipating the buzz of all the riders and their horses when I got there. The traffic was heavy on the freeway, but I turned up my radio and sang along to the alternative music playing on Triple J, the government funded national radio station that I liked. I loved the randomness of the station, the songs they played, the way they supported local artists and the fact that it was advertising free!

When I arrived at the Centre I felt upbeat and alive, and parked my car near the float. Luckily there was space for my car, and I could easily back onto it. For now though I was excited and wanted to find my horse and to let Gail and Crystal know I was here early. So I left the car unhooked and went in search.

Bundy Bear wasn't anywhere to be seen in the stables, I looked for Gail and Crustal and they weren't anywhere either. I searched the grassed areas, just in case he was being taken for a walk and eating grass. Nothing. I walked towards the arenas where there were some horses and looked for Bundy.

As I made my way around the centre, I sent a text to Tom to say where I was. Then I saw him in the jump arena. Crystal was riding him around and around, jumping him over the fences that were about 120cm high. I stood and watched some distance away, so she had no idea I was there. She cantered around and around, over and over the jumps. I walked up a bit closer, and noticed she had an ear piece in with a cord going to her pocket. Then Bundy Bear jumped a jump and dropped the top rail. As he did, I saw Gail run in to pick it up. Crystal spoke into her ear piece. I realised she was on the phone, probably to her coach. For the next thirty minutes, I stood and watched, they were unaware I was there.

As my stomach churned and my heart beat fast, I moved around the arena to a space they could see me. I watched as Bundy Bear started to pant, and was now getting a big sweat up, and yet it wasn't a hot day. I walked up to a hill and sat down, trying to be still and work out what was actually going on. They continued to put the jumps up and she continued to canter him and jump him. Not once in the time I was there watching, did she stop him, walk him or rest in any way. It was over and over. I had knots in my stomach and I hated it.

"You think she would let him rest" I said to the lady beside me, as I became agitated.

She turned and acknowledged me but said nothing. I watched quietly for another ten minutes; then couldn't take it anymore. My phone was still in my car and I needed to talk to Tom. I walked off towards the car breaking into a run, and tears started to run down my cheeks. I dialled the number, but by the time he answered I was a sobbing mess. "What's the matter" asked Tom "are you hurt?"

"No I'm OK, but Bundy Bear – she is just riding him and jumping and riding and jumping. He is sweating and he hates it"

"Tell her to get off him, or to at least rest him."

"I can't, I've given him to her to ride."

"Yes you can, he is still your horse." Tom said quickly. "Do it now."

"But," I started as I felt the tips of my ears burning.

"Now! Amanda, you need to stop her from wrecking your horse. Take control." I felt wrong as I had lent her my horse, but I had been conflicted by what she was doing to him.

I hung up the phone, sucked in my breath and walked back with purpose in my step.

As I neared the arena I called to Gail, "Gail could you ask her to rest please?" I said it strongly but not aggressively.

Gail flung around and her eyes widened. She yelled at me, "How dare you tell us what to do!"

"Gail" I started, and softly said, "he is my horse."

She turned and yelled abuse at me, her arms were flailing, and she was spitting words out with vehemence. The words tumbled over me in shock, but I didn't hear all of them. Something about how dare I, wrecking a child's dream, interfering. I stopped listening.

Crystal had got off him, and I was walking him back to the stables to unsaddle him.

As I got to his stable area I took off his bridle, there was another lady from her team there and she saw the blood in his mouth. "This is disgusting," I said, and she walked over to see what I was talking about.

"Look at this blood, she's ripped his mouth" I said, lifting his lips to inspect the area.

"That's not good," she said, but then turned and walked away quickly.

I placed his head collar on and thought to myself I had asked her to rest him, and this was the result. What was actually going on?

As I walked Bundy Bear away, I looked at him. He had blood coming from his mouth, he was hot and heaving. I saw Gail running over towards the official's tent. I stopped looking at what else they did. My concentration was on my horse.

As I untacked him, I noticed the cuts in his mouth, and why the blood was coming out. I was a sobbing mess. How could someone have done this to my horse?

I decided he was coming home with me tonight and there was nothing they could do about it. I took his saddle off, and then I saw the welts behind it. Two huge welts that were in the place of where spurs would rest. She had been wearing spurs on him and they had dug in so bad they were causing him to welt.

I hugged his neck and said I was so sorry. My eyes were sore from crying as I hosed him down to try and cool him and walked him around near the floats - away from where the riders and their teams were. I called Tom and told him what had happened. He was bewildered, but happy I was bringing him home tonight.

Some random man came and helped me hook the float up, and helped me gather my saddle and bridle. The night air had started to chill and I placed a rug over his still wet body. Still crying I loaded Bundy Bear up and closed the back of the float. "I have to get my act together," I said to him "I've got to drive home, and for that I need to see," I smiled and mouthed thank you to the man. As I was getting ready to leave, Gail came flying around the corner, yelling more abuse at me.

"I'm taking him home, Gail. And the more you throw those words at me, the less likely I will be bringing him back again tomorrow." I said as I unlocked the car. "Good bye."

She was still yelling as I pulled away.

I drove out of the centre and towards home. I was numb. It wasn't for a good few kilometres before I breathed. I wanted to run into Tom's arms and for him to tell me all would be okay. I wanted my horse to be okay, and not be damaged. I don't remember the drive home.

I got Bundy Bear off the float and placed him in his stable. Tom had put the lights on, so I could check him over. I took his rig off, and the welts had grown, they started to look nasty. His mouth was swollen but he had stopped bleeding.

I gave him a hug, a warm rug and said a prayer to him, wishing him a good night.

The phone calls had started whilst I drove home, but I had ignored them. By the time everything was settled in the stables, there was nine missed calls, and a dozen texts from Gail. The final one telling me her husband was driving all his gear back to us tonight, and Bundy Bear was no longer needed. They had sourced a better horse. My blood boiled. I was furious at the insinuation that he was not a good horse. At what they had done to him, at the way she had reacted to me, and that Bundy Bear was dropped. I was totally confused as Tom saw me and took me in his welcoming arms. "I'm so sorry darling," he said as he led Bundy Bear into the stables. Once we knew he was settled, he said, "come inside I've got some dinner ready for you, or would you prefer a glass of wine now and dinner later?"

Wiping away tears, I replied "wine" and sat down on the coach with a thump.

An hour or so later, we saw the headlights of a car coming up the drive. We both walked outside to see the father had arrived. I had forgotten his name but couldn't talk anyway, so it made no difference. I helped him unload the gear in silence. I didn't thank him for driving up, I wanted to ask him why he lived with his wife. But I didn't. I wanted to ask him many things, and make comments about what I'd witnessed. But I didn't.

He drove off the property, and I breathed a sigh of relief.

The next day, Bundy Bear was in a bad way. He wouldn't eat his food, his sides looked terrible, and he hung his head. His mouth was swollen and scabs had formed where the cuts were. A horse's mouth normally heals quickly, but this looked like it was getting worse. I called the vet and he came to inspect him. He gave me some drugs to calm his nerves, antibiotics to stop any infection forming on the sores in his mouth and told me to monitor him. Bundy stood for hours with his head hanging and not moving; his energy was heavy, and there was sadness in his whole being.

Within a week, the hair had fallen off the lesions on his sides, his mouth was slowly healing, but it still looked bad. He wasn't eating, he was losing weight, and I was starting to panic. It appeared his pain was so strong he was shutting down.

I called a holistic vet to come and see what he would say. Dr Bruce was an equine veterinarian who specialised in acupuncture and holistic medicines. I met Dr Bruce and his assistant Christine and they both looked at Bundy Bear. Bruce lifted the lips to see the colour of his gums. They were black, not pink or red, or white, they were black. Like he had been eating liquorice. But he hadn't.

They looked at one another, but said nothing. Dr Bruce did his acupuncture as I held onto Bundy Bear's lead rope. They murmured something between themselves but I didn't catch it. Christine wrote her notes. After an hour of therapy, Dr Bruce said to me, "now this horse needs your love. He needs to know that you love him," odd I thought, how many vets say that to you. "Oh I do," I replied.

"He also needs these Chinese herbs. Give one teaspoon in his feed morning and night," he said.

"That's great – keep telling him how much you love him. I'll come back in a week. I've done all I can for now. If anything changes for the worse, call me straight away. Otherwise I'll see you in a week." He said as he started to pack his tools back into his car. They jumped into the car and drove off.

I stood and cuddled Bundy Bear for about twenty minutes.

For the next week I told him I loved him, I fed him, gave him his Chinese medicine and watched as he didn't get worse, but he didn't get better.

Dr Bruce and Christine came back as promised. I watched as they both got out of the car. "Oh he's alive." said Dr Bruce. "Yes he's alive" I said thinking he was having a joke.

He went straight into diagnosing and treating again.

After another hour of watching the changes take place with the acupuncture and use of pressure points finally Dr Bruce spoke.

"I didn't think he was going to survive last week," he said turning to me.

"His black mouth indicated that he was about to die. I've actually never seen a horse that bad, and I'm pleased to say I've now witnessed one come back to life. He was in a bad state."

I stood and listened, aghast. I had no idea what to say or how to respond.

He handed me some more Chinese herbs, and reassured me that Bundy was on the mend.

All his gear was thrown in a pile in the tack room. I hadn't walked in there since he had returned home. I was in a bad way. I hated that someone had damaged my horse so much, with such total disregard. I nursed Bundy Bear back to health over the next six months. He was in a bad way.

I never heard from anyone, not even the organising committee. I was empty and didn't trust the horse world or people who said they were authorities.

For Bundy Bear, it was a traumatic event. His brain had been wired to process that event as something to avoid at all costs. As a prey animal he needed to stay safe, and it is likely this traumatic memory will stay with him for the rest of his days. His whole life routine that we had painstakingly built had altered. There were new stimuli that would cause new triggers, and much more work was needed.

There were times when I wanted to be able to focus on him making a physical recovery, yet it was more than that, it was a mental recovery that was also needed.

He became depressed, just as he had been when I first met him. It appeared that trust had gone, he didn't trust me, or others. I hated the way he was and tried to think horse, and what he wanted. So I made it important for Bundy Bear to feel his family around him, and for him to continue to live his identity as a feisty, strong minded yet loving horse. He didn't though, he had lost that identity along with his weight and strength.

I wondered if he wanted to share his energy and connection with the other horses so that he was able to process his healing. But he stood in the paddock with his head down and looked very sad. I would come home from work and go out in the paddock to see how he was. I tried to get him to eat by handpicking grasses. He would nibble them and then just stand and hold his head half way down. So I'd try giving him experiences that he once enjoyed, including a scratch behind his ears or lengthy grooming and hosing sessions. I knew that touch is connecting, and bonding and that they were healing for him and myself. I needed the touch, and felt he did too.

For weeks I watched him, and held him and tried to get him to move from his misery. It was an emotional and also challenging time for both Tom and me as well as the horses. As I moved through the tough times, the hardship and immense grief, I tried to be there for him. Tom supported me in ways to show that he was there. We kept working and going through each day one step at a time. The impact on the family was huge, yet if we mentioned it to anyone they would not understand. Even close friends who I thought knew how powerful he was. It seemed we lived this misery by ourselves. At times, I wondered if I was dreaming up this amazing horse, if he was just in my imagination. Was I the only one who could see his brilliance, and now his sadness? Was he just part of our world, and no one else wanted to see it?

During this time, I also realised I needed to heal myself from the pain and grief the events brought up and I needed to be kind to me. I found it was so therapeutic to make a little time for myself, and to gently remind myself that I didn't need to blame or give myself a hard time. I had to really be truly authentic and know that I had a right to feel and express my inner self. Even though it was truly hard, I knew that lessons will be learnt and my authentic self will become deeper and stronger and richer for the experience.

Day after day, I watched as this once vibrant and open horse became a small, closed, sad horse. He didn't want to be ridden, he hardly ate, and he didn't want to be part of anything; he lost weight, or wouldn't put on anything. I started to realise that maybe I would never compete with him again. Maybe he was so broken he would remain in my paddock to live out his days.

It was a long six months before I could see any change in Bundy

Bear. He wasn't recovered, but he was on the way to recovery and whatever that looked like for him. This time was needed for me to also process and work through what had happened, and to gain momentum to move forward with purpose again. During this whole time, his gear had remained crumpled as it had been delivered the night of his return. I couldn't face it, nor put it away. And for now it wasn't needed. My horse had been dying and I needed him to live.

One day, when I was feeling I was up to putting away his gear, I got out his bridle. It had been shortened by 4 holes each side by the rider or her mother. That meant it was ridiculously tight in his mouth. The noseband had also been shortened and tightened. It sickened me to look at it and I threw it against the side of the room in disgust. "How dare they!!" I bellowed. "They tried to kill my horse with their mismanagement". I dropped my head into my hands and closed my eyes and bawled my eyes out. When I was done, there was nothing left in me to think about the cruelty of these people. No words would come. No wonder he had blood in his mouth on the night I collected him, and then those horrid scars on the side of his mouth, that had taken so many weeks to heal.

Slowly, he started to regain some of himself back again. He was eating with the herd, and had even taken up being the leader again. That quiet leader who said nothing, but everyone followed. As he progressed through his recovery I decided it was time to hop on his back again and see how he went. I didn't put a saddle on him, instead I mounted him bareback, and only had him in a halter, rather than being bridled. I never wanted to put a bit in his mouth again.

As I rode him around the paddock, I felt he was accepting of me being there, but I could feel there was still no passion, no bounce and frivolity as he had always had. He plodded along and did what he did, but there was no spark. I took him out on the bush trails a couple of times a week, and started to practise some fun in hand games in the arena to rebuild that mutual joy and trust, all the while being mindful of his sore mouth and tenderness behind the saddle.

I went with my instinct day by day, and took it one day at a time, keeping the joy and his fear within his comfort zone. I breathed deeply, and I allowed us both time. Sometimes it felt just not right to ride and I didn't. There was no pressure from me or my family, and I wouldn't accept any judgments from others. This was our own journey and I was responsible for all of the decisions I made, whether they were good or bad. For me, there is no greater sense of accomplishment than turning that fear and trauma into feelings of safety, relaxation, and trust.

With spring, our life journey revealed a new gratitude for both of us. I noticed the smallest actions of kindness, the flowers, the song of the birds, the sun peeping through the trees in between the showers, the rebirth of plants, the roar of the ocean and the healing of the natural world.

The heat of the summer allowed us to ride or be together in the early hours when it wasn't so hot. This meant getting up super early to enable me to go into work afterwards. Some days, I would ride him out in the bush, and it was on one early morning that I noticed a change. In the past, when he was out in the bush he would stick to paths and be really happy trotting or cantering along them. This day he didn't. He wanted to stop and smell. He was looking at plants, smelling them and then tasting them. It seemed to be a whole visceral experience. Even though I had to get to work, I was happy to just let him explore, and for me to watch and listen. It was intriguing to notice him behaving this way. I was curious about what he was doing, and why. "What are you doing, mate? Is that beneficial, is it healing?" I'd ask, but of course he never answered me.

He would walk into the bush, stop and then taste different plants. Sometimes staying for a while as he ate the whole plant. I felt into my body and got the sense he was nurturing some sense of youth. A sense that he was going back to his childhood, as a young horse. He seemed to be happy, and in fact opening up to the sensations that were coming. This was good for me to feel this, as I knew for many months he had been closed down to all sensations. I felt we were on the path to improvement.

It was during the cooler days at the end of summer that he started to take on his role again in the Equine Assisted Learning sessions. I had a group of people where we were working, honing their communication skills and building healthier relationships. As the group stood in the paddock I noticed Bundy Bear walking up and observing. This time he was willing to be part of the herd, where for many months he had stood back and not even watched. I am a facilitator who lets my horses choose if they wish to participate, and so for me this was his choice and I respected that. He started to be that strength again, not as powerful as he once was, yet I could see it coming out. I could feel it inside me.

When working with humans and animals, I was mindful that every situation and being is unique. Every perspective is our own personal "learning curve." And especially when it comes to the partnership with my horses, no one knows better than how I feel inside.

On that day, he provided a non-judgmental zone for all, and I knew things were starting to mend. And just as he helped others, they helped him. He started to look up, and be willing to go out. He started to stand his ground in the paddock, just like he had always done. Was he out of the woods, I wondered, maybe not yet, but he was going in a positive direction.

As winter set in and I still wasn't riding him out of the property, or to any competitions, I started to miss them. This was the time of year when the season was in full swing. I knew each event, and when it landed in the calendar, and where we had travelled years before. I was sad and maybe if I was truthful, lonely. I missed going out and being with others in the competition environment. I missed talking horses to like-minded people.

BEING TOGETHER

The mere act of being together shall bestow upon souls a profound tranquillity and serenity.

There were days when I would spend sometimes up to an hour just being with the horses. I would stand between the herd and just "be" there with them. I wouldn't actually do anything other than relaxing and watching them while they ate. When I entered the paddock and stood with them, I would find they became sleepy eyed and would lower their heads for a long time. During these times, I would stay until they decided it was time to leave. When one would finally begin to munch grass and step away the others would follow, and that would be my pass to go.

This calm in the paddock was something that couldn't be found elsewhere and it helped me to relax after the hustle of everyday. Was it the sound of their breathing or chewing? Was it the methodical eating movement of the horses as they quietly moved from patch to patch? Or the occasional swish of a tail? It was this place where I felt deep within me the contentedness of the horses as they grazed the grasses.

I loved this time just being with my horses - no expectations, no agenda, and no rush. I felt like we were all part of the same herd, and my heart would be so peaceful after that time. The feeling of well-being and abundance would enshroud me. It was that same feeling I had when I was travelling the world a few years earlier. A feeling that was not always present in my busy, city driven life.

Through this mindful intention and actually allowing myself to enjoy the process, things changed. It was like I needed to take one step backwards so I could take two steps forward, to keep me healthy and on my right path in life. Instead of ploughing through life and then being forced to slow down by some mysterious illness or burn out, I was taking time to grow incrementally.

The horses had helped me to realise that an essential part of my day was the need to be taking a step back and asking, why the rush? What am I actually working towards? It helped so much with my relationships.

I noticed when I practised replenishing my physical and emotional energy with the horses, that there was actually little correlation with the hours that I put into my work day, and the actual tasks I could accomplish. That in itself was gold to me. In fact, I started to notice that when I took more time off to be with the horses, I achieved twice as much as I did before. I was convinced that it wasn't the quantity of hours I put towards my productivity, but rather the quality.

I learnt to do things that filled me up. To notice when I was feeling overly tired or starting to doubt myself, my behaviour changed immediately. I set limits on the amount of time I spent reading emails and taking calls from colleagues and clients. It was my priority. It was a shift in my perspective.

This change of perspective allowed me to be a better communicator at work. I was able to buffer negative comments.

The horses would show me ways towards peaceful contemplation. They help me see what it is, to have no worries about tomorrow, that there is no need to rush and no regrets about yesterday, just as they do. This is what's really important in life. I was encouraged through their interactions to slow down and enjoy the simple pleasures of pure contentment. To listen to what I know in my heart is right and not what others want me to do.

Bundy has allowed me to see that when I am stuck and at a crossroads with my horse or even a human, that the best solution is to listen. Listen to my body and my 'knowing' in my mind and body. Now I know when someone tells me what I should do and what's right, then I wait for my intuition, that inner "knowing" to tell me if I should decide otherwise.

I now know that often in life there is no "right or wrong." That I have previous experiences and things that might work better in some situations. And just because I have experienced something bad doesn't mean that the same situation will always end up bad too.

I'm human.

I make mistakes.

Mistakes that come from years of Germanic rule when I was a kid, rules that Mum thought would help us in life, rules that she had learnt as she grew up in war torn Holland, rules that kept her and her family safe. Yet in Australia, maybe they weren't applicable. I learnt behaviours that served me well when I was a kid, but not so much anymore - now that I am older, and wiser, well a bit wiser anyway. I have a choice to make my own decisions.

I'm emotional, I cry…lots. I get angry and I know I have shit happening that needs to be resolved. BUT I have a horse that helps me, guides me and steers me into directions that once I'd never step into.

When I was travelling after I finished school, I learnt so much about myself. I learnt ways to deal with situations but mostly I learnt a lot about myself. I know I grew up in the time I was away from the corporate world. And I understood my strengths and weaknesses as well as where my limits were. How I actually knew the answers was when I stopped to listen. I loved travelling by myself, I also sometimes felt a bit of FOMO, but I had strategies to work with that - like booking into a hostel and meeting other travellers. When I wanted to be alone, I would choose a room in someone's private house. Travelling alone took me out of my comfort zone, and so I had to learn to adapt to the change and uncertainty. I got to do new things, eat new food, meet new people, and learn new languages or accents, and cultures. I was intuitive, and an introvert. I got a chance to not worry about anything and focus on my passions; all the things I am capable of doing. It truly was a life-changing experience for me.

Yet, when I stepped back into the corporate world, and got caught on that treadmill of hustle, I forgot all of that. I got caught in the endless quest for more. I started to chase titles, achievements, promotions and money. I did more, went to more places, made more progress, but I felt less. These stresses and strains of working for prolonged durations appeared, and my mental health deteriorated gradually.

I led from a place of ego, and power, at home, in the yard and at work. It probably originated from my Dutch stock where we spoke our mind and demanded action. My childhood was strict and actionable so I knew nothing better at that time of my life and translated that into being a leader in the workplace. Yet, I soon found that outdated top-down leadership was very counterproductive. I focused too much on control and end goals, thus I made it very difficult to achieve my own desired outcomes. Slowly, over time, I learnt this was not effective and upon reflection it cost me both staff and business dealings. It also stressed me out, and caused me to become very sick at one point.

When I finally finished work for the day, I would rush out to the yards, ride my horse and come inside to wine, and spend the evening watching TV that helped me to relax. Then the next day I would do it all over again. It seemed that everywhere I went, people were suffering from this hustle culture, to work harder, stronger, faster. To do more, and to tell others how much you did. I wanted to sedate myself to the madness through wine and distraction. I had created a monster rushing around to be seen to be doing the right thing. Whatever that was. Self-care was not even an afterthought.

It wasn't until Bundy Bear came into my life that I started on my journey of personal growth, being mindfully aware and finding authentic leadership. Bundy Bear reminded me about the art of resting and relaxing and that it helps in preventing the onset of illnesses, helps clear my mind, focus, to find my creativity and solutions to problems. It started slowly and grew as I realised the impact of what I was changing, how I was communicating and how happy I and my life and my work team had become.

When I started changing my habits, I would stop and listen during the day and it was this that made a huge difference. Yet, still I would hear those voices that told me it was a waste of time. "What are you doing this for? You've got things to do..." I thought this was wasted time, and I needed to get on with her life as a business leader, a wife, and a rider.

Bundy Bear sensed how I felt on a given day and tried to calm me down when I felt too anxious or stressed. Over time I learnt to slow down and to enjoy. Then I made it part of my ritual, to bring myself to the moment, to pause, and to remove the stresses of the day. This pause, rather than taking time away, seemed to have an opposite effect, it enabled me to achieve more!

Our partnership has grown substantially in our four-and-a-half years together. In that time we had experienced bush rides, beach rides, dressage wins, eventing wins and lots of communication. We had shared many moments of peace, of mistakes and triumphs. We had overcome obstacles together, faced our fears and shared determination. He has been my teacher, and mentor and I have also taught him and guided him. We shared our path together.

I have learned to embrace my childlike self, and listen to the innocent, ever righteous horse that was changing my life for the better.

As our partnership grew, Bundy and I grew, and we experienced more together. I started to raise my expectations of him and our work together. He has shown me over the years that he is not always in the same space mentally, and with that our growth is definitely not linear. There are times where I just have to take a step back and go back to basics. Bundy Bear is the greatest leveller.

My riding has changed, I now ask more questions of each horse, and when I get an answer from them I consider it, and how I'm going to respond. There is no pushing, bullying or arguing. There are lots of questions and lots of listening. We talk continually. It's taken a lot of effort and a fair amount of time, yet Bundy has progressed from a being a shutdown, timid, stressed horse that was disinterested in people, struggling with a lack of confidence, to becoming a loving, affectionate and confident horse that tries to help his rider out - even when I'm not performing at my best. He loves a good face rub, especially on his eyes. He smiles at me, yawns when satisfied, and even laughs at my jokes. He holds me in his space when I cry, and lets me be myself.

It has taken giving him a voice, establishing a bond, listening and a lot of love and attention (plus a fair number of treats and massages) for me to get that very first welcome whinny. Now that whinny is regularly shared with me and that makes it all worth the effort. He has become my peace and I have become his human. Bundy has given me the motivation, the courage and the strength to believe I can succeed. He has helped me with my outlook on life and the way I interact with others. He has helped me to be a better human in all the aspects of my life.

No matter how hard I try, I know I will never lose him as a horse friend. I feel Bundy's love without any conditions and know that he values my care and time.

WORK

Self-discovery is a transformative shift, altering the very perception one holds of their own being.

These transformations had a profound impact on my perspective toward work. Initially, when I joined the department, it was in disarray, lacking proper processes and systems. Collaboration was lacking, and not everyone put in a full day's work. However, by developing my emotional awareness, I gained the assertiveness and motivation to bring about changes.

I dedicated time to understand the business and the required systems, implementing them effectively. Through this journey, I witnessed significant changes within myself. At first, I would question why certain things hadn't been done before and seek permission from my Director. But he always empowered me to make decisions on my own. Over time, I realised that I needed to take the initiative and implement the changes myself. Only after completing them would I discuss with my Director the reasons, the methods, and the outcomes of the changes.

The day I stopped and listened to Bundy Bear as we rode out in the bush was the day I drove to work considering my boredom. Was it a warning telling me I wasn't doing what I wanted to be doing? Or was it the 'push' that I needed to motivate me to switch goals and projects?

By the time I got into work, I had realised that my team, the company, and possibly even my systems and products had become boring. I walked into my Directors office and told him, hoping I could move to another role within the business. I put my case forward and asked if there were any roles that he could see me doing. Not being one to say too much, he smiled and thanked me for coming in, and said he'd be in touch.

I wanted to embrace my boredom, rather than avoiding it, and I wanted to stop and listen instead becoming more removed from my current responsibilities. I looked at the impact I'd made on others in the team, our stakeholders and the benefits for the business. I considered the recipients of the changes I'd made, and the positive aspect for them. This got me thinking about what else I could do, and the possibilities of going out and being a consultant. I started to plan what that looked like, and how I would go about it. I planned to resign in one months' time, around spring. My boss had other ideas – he called me into his office a week later and gave me a redundancy, telling me he had just been told they needed to cut numbers, and when I had came to him and said I was bored, I saved his bacon!

I was walked out the door immediately, and told never to contact anyone again, especially not my team. I drove home in shock. As I parked my car, I walked straight out to the paddock to be with Bundy Bear and tell him how shit I felt. I wanted someone to hear the pain, the feelings. I poured it all out. I felt like I'd been given the sack, I felt like failure personified, and that I'd been wronged and told off. By being involuntarily forced to leave my position, rather than choosing to do it myself, was swirling me into a blizzard of emotion: embarrassment, shame, worthlessness, self-pity, and depression. To say I was shocked and taken by surprise was an understatement. My identity had been deeply embedded with what I did, as a leader, and in my industry. So getting terminated was fast becoming one of my life's most stressful and devastating events. That and Bundy Bear not having fully recovered had me spiralling into a big black hole.

Even though I wanted to start my own consultancy, at this point I was not capable. I sat out on the decking overlooking the paddocks, drinking a cup of tea, and considering who I was. I felt shit. It didn't matter how positive I was trying to be, it still rocked me. No matter how much I tried, I couldn't just pick myself up, dust myself off, and bounce back. No one was going to hire someone who was feeling sorry for herself. It had hurt my self-esteem in ways I was not expecting.

So, just as I had with Bundy Bear, I allowed myself time to relax, eating ice-cream when I felt like it and staying in my pyjamas till just before Tom came home. Whilst I was filled with self-judgement, anger, and shame I needed to give myself the time to grieve the loss of my job, and the leader status. I allowed myself to grieve the familiar daily routine of working, the loss of interactions with former colleagues, and the sense of purpose that my work gave me. Whilst I knew I needed to move on, I wasn't ready just yet. There were complicated emotions that I needed to process and just when I thought I'd finished with one, another would come along. Whilst the ice-cream helped with these changes of emotions, there were times when all I wanted to do was sulk and feel sorry for myself.

Eric, the family white and black spotted Bull Mastiff came over and laid his head on my lap. His jowls felt like he'd just had a drink of water. He looked up at me with his doleful eyes. It looked like he didn't want me to sit around acting sad for long. As he lifted his head, he left behind a very wet patch on my jeans. "Thanks Eric," I said as he turned and walked away.

When I looked at socials I felt envious of others who had work and I compared myself to those who had started their own business. I couldn't even go out and compete on my horse to help myself move on. So, in one of my lowest moments I knew I needed to do something different. I stopped scrolling through social media and tried to stop thinking about what everyone else is doing, and just focus on me.

As I sat there looking at the horses in the paddock I let the tears, pain and grieving roll.

Whether it was Eric's disdain for my pity party or the actual time that I had sat around feeling sorry for myself, I could feel a change in me. I was on the decking with my laptop open, searching job adverts and pondering my life when my new phone rang. It was Tony, one of my ex-team members.

"Hey," I said sadly as he announced who he was.

"I've been worried about you since the day you were sacked. Well we all have really, but because they took your phone, no one knew how to contact you," he said.

"Thanks, it's been pretty shit really," I said.

"Yeah. They didn't even allow you to go back to your office, or say goodbye to anyone! We've packed up your office and put it into boxes. I wondered if you wanted me to come up and give them to you." Tony asked kindly.

Tears pricked my eyes as his sympathetic words sunk in.

"I, I don't know" I stammered.

"Look I'm heading out to Northam a bit later, and I can swing past your place on my way. It's no trouble, and anyway I think we need a coffee," He said.

"Okay" was all I could say as my mouth was closing up. I cleared my throat and said, "see you later then" and hung up the phone.

He arrived an hour later, and by that time I had changed out of my pyjamas and put the kettle on. Placing cake onto a tray, along with cups and the sugar bowl, I walked outside. As he brought the two boxes filled with my possessions, I looked on. Tony is a 40 something big man. He's been around the traps, and I was actually surprised to see him here.

"Hey, thanks for coming" I said, putting down the tray on the outside table.

"No worries," he replied "Oh gosh I didn't expect cake, thanks you're a saint, and know me well. I was going to stop at the Bakery and pick something up, but I got delayed at work, and wanted to keep going."

"All good. This cake is fresh, I think you'll like it. How did you get my number?" I asked him.

"Let's say I did some digging around, and you had given it to Belinda from resources, so she gave it to me," he said with a twinkle in his eye. I got the feeling he was well pleased with himself.

"Oh yeah, I forgot I'd given it to her," I replied drily. Why was I being such a jerk? I wanted to be happy he was here, but all I could think of was how the team were talking about me, I imagined they felt sorry for me – me the failure, retrenched and dismissed.

"It was important that I came out to see you, not just to give you these boxes. We all feel really bad for what they did to you, Amanda. You were seriously the best boss we've ever had. You listened to us, you thought about different ways, and you gave us reason to come to work. We were trusted, and given responsibility, plus you had implemented a brilliant system for the team."

Wow, I thought, I certainly didn't expect to hear that!

"Thanks," I wanted to cry, but instead lifted my lips to form a smile, not sure it actually reached my eyes, but I was trying to make some happiness appear on my face as I looked at him.

"So, I'm here from all the team, and hope you are okay," Tony said as he stirred sugar into his coffee.

"I'm not really. I think it shook me," I blurted out wishing I hadn't. This was a team member, ex-team member. In fact I realised right then, that I no longer had to be his boss. I could be real.

We spoke some more about the pain and grieving process I had gone through. He listened and encouraged me, he didn't argue, debate, or contradict. I didn't defend myself or blame my boss. We just talked. And he paid attention to me. It was a challenging exercise, but I knew it was serving me well. By the time he had finished the cake and coffee, he was ready to leave and I actually felt better.

Tony had given me a gift. A gift of hearing me, and allowing me to be me.

Later that day, I realised that being terminated didn't define me, my capabilities, or my future career any more than it did anyone else. Just like Bundy Bear had shown he needed time to do his processing, I also needed time. Just not lots of time, I thought to myself smiling.

So when I woke the next morning and felt the sensations of being excited about what lay ahead, I knew I was on the mend. I lay in bed and listened to the magpies as they chortled outside my bedroom window. The visit from Tony had reminded me to reach out and purposefully share my positive energy rather than tuning into my own place of fear. So, intentionally I would add gratitude to my day, starting with a thank you to my former Director when I was ready. I gathered myself and dressed, ready to go out into the stables.

Bundy Bear was there waiting for me. That was a good sign, I thought. At least he's keen to embrace life. I threw him some hay, and raced back inside to put my jodhpurs on along with a suitable top for hanging around dirty horses. Bundy Bear always loved to rub his eyes on my shirt, so there was no point in having a clean shirt on. He was still in the yards eating his hay when I returned. I grabbed a head collar and saddled him up. As I put the saddle on him, I felt his energy - as if there was anything he needed me to know. There was excitement, a good feeling for where I was. I took him to the mounting block, got on and took him out the back gate to the bush for a ride. As we got to the gate, Eric came racing over, huffing with his huge jowls and doing a little dance. He was certainly excited to be going out again. It had been some time, I thought. He looked up at me and almost smiled, a big toothy, jowly smile only a Bull Mastiff can do. I smiled back. "Thanks Eric," I said out loud.

As we wove down the path from the gate Eric trotted along beside us. It was a beautiful morning, and I actually realised that with all of my sadness, I had missed this time of the day. The time when I was alone in the bush with my horse and dog. We ambled through the bushland, Bundy picking his feet over logs and rocks as we wove our way up a hilltop behind our place. I love this place I thought as I breathed in the strong scent of eucalyptus. Bundy turned to look in the distance, and I followed his gaze to see a mob of roos. The kangaroos stood around in a group on their powerful hind legs, their long, strong tail on the ground and as we approached, I saw their small front legs lift. They lifted their heads to see if they needed to bounce off, and decided they were heading down the valley away from us. I looked for Eric, and was grateful when I saw him off in the opposite direction. Hopefully, he didn't see them I thought as I knew if he threatened them then they could rear up on their hind legs and kick out. These kicks can rip the hide off the dog. I watched them bound away as I saw a female kangaroo with a bulging pouch on her belly. I knew it contained her joey. I decided to ensure Eric didn't see them. I would go in the other direction, and so I turned down the hill, and trotted away over a fallen log. The burst of pace got Bundy Bear excited and he cantered off, loving the time to blow out some air. We cantered through the scrubs until we got to the path, and then he took off in a gallop, I leant forward and let him go. Once he had blown out all of the cobwebs we came back to a walk to cool down. I laughed at him, patting his now hot neck. "Well done and thanks mate," I said to him.

Tom was on shift work doing some huge IT rollout, and so I didn't have much time with him. When he was home he slept, and it seemed we had limited time together. As the birds woke me the next morning I rolled over to see I was alone again. I got up and swallowed my pride, then sat down at the computer to write an email to my former Director, thanking him for the opportunity to work in the organisation and offering my assistance should he ever need help in the future. I knew this process was key to mastering my new found positivity.

This was the first step of many that would enable me to move forward into the new chapter of my life.

AUTHOR'S NOTE.

If there's one thing I've learned throughout my journey with horses, it's that I am a winner not because I possess innate greatness as a rider or a leader; it's because I value the journey itself and I'm open to embracing different ways of being. Whenever I approach my work with the expectation of immediate results, the process tends to stagnate. However, when I focus on the horse in front of me today, even if it feels like I'm taking a step back from yesterday, it doesn't mean that progress isn't happening. The same applies to working with my staff; if I can simply accept the horse or person in the present moment, without attaching myself to where I think we should be, the desired outcomes will naturally emerge.

I've come to realise that results may not always come easily or within the expected timeframe. However, by striving for success, actively listening, and continuously improving, I have witnessed the payoff over time. Patience has been a crucial element in achieving the results I've been seeking. This doesn't mean that life is always smooth sailing. Challenges and unexpected circumstances do arise, but when I pause and truly listen, the desired results eventually manifest. Building strong relationships is vital on this path. My values now revolve around the process itself, maintaining a sense of curiosity, and embracing the joy of each moment.

That is why I am able to share my life the way it is today. My beliefs and values have changed so much. Where once I was a goal-oriented, stressed, angry, often confused, sometimes unhappy go-getter, I am no longer that person today. Where I believed the universe and all beings are connected, today I know it is true and that the energy and beliefs that we send out can influence other circumstances. Each day is a journey to me, and as I have no idea how much more time I am given on this earth I want to make it worthwhile and enjoy the learning, the being, the process, the journey. It is a process of creation, not of the destination.

I never stop learning from my horses. I lead from doing, and practise leading from a sense of peace, yet with structure. The way I am with my horses helps me as I work on myself. That leadership enables me to help others so that they can awaken their natural awareness and live and work with more authentic relationships and connections. My competence is a continuous journey as the more I know the more I realise I actually don't know because my horse will tell me. The horse is always the best barometer of when I am getting something right. Yet, I now realise that I am figuring out "my way" in this journey of life and this crazy world we live in.

Bundy Bear is all about communication and sharing his skills with others. He knows the pain of being hurt, being ignored, and not being loved. Together, we also found out about true love, and enjoying each day. Now that is where he belongs in the world, he is strong and knows he can communicate, so he has a huge message to share. In this book you have read of many of his wise methods, and experienced them through my words. At shows, when attending the local Riding Club and in the paddock, Bundy leaves a mark on all who meet him, and it is our wish that we share these insights to help you in your life.

It is from those years of being with this wise horse that this story on life and how to live it, came about. The change took time, many years, with many tales along the way. As I watched him change and listened to him, I came to realise that he also helped me. When I truly listened I was astounded by how "talkative" he actually was once he realised I was paying attention!

While in the presence of this amazing horse what I felt was becoming more important to me than what I thought. When I tuned into this feeling, it was powerful. I realised that he was responding to my non-verbal communication as an individual, including my true emotions and feelings. He held no judgement, yet there were times where he would 'mirror' my own emotions back to me in his demonstrated behaviour.

This new way of being has enabled me to focus my time and energy on helping others, as well as my horse.

NOTES

1. BUNDY'S STORY

1. https://en.wikipedia.org/wiki/Clydesdale_horse
2. https://www.nma.gov.au/exhibitions/defining-symbols-australia/billy#:~:text=The%20billy%20is%20an%20Australian,the%20kangaroo%20and%20the%20wattle.
3. Breaking a horse means to train it to accept a rider and respond to commands, typically through the use of a saddle and bridle.
4. https://en.wikipedia.org/wiki/Road_train

2. MELANIE

1. Dressage is a type of equestrian sport that involves the horse and rider performing a series of predetermined movements in response to subtle cues from the rider. Dressage is a highly skilled and elegant form of horse riding and training that is often referred to as "horse ballet." It is an equestrian sport that showcases the harmonious partnership between a rider and their horse. The word "dressage" is derived from the French term "dresser," which means "to train."
2. Although horses are traditionally measured in hands, with Europeanisation horses are also measured in centimetres.
3. A gelding is a term used to refer to a castrated male horse. This procedure is typically done to control the horse's behaviour, as geldings tend to be calmer and easier to handle than stallions or mares. Geldings are commonly used for riding, driving, and various equestrian activities due to their more predictable and manageable nature.

www.ingramcontent.com/pod-product-compliance
Lightning Source LLC
Chambersburg PA
CBHW070250010526
44107CB00056B/2411